PROMISES FROM GOD'S WORD

Spiritual, Devotional, Inspirational & Motivational

DR. JOHN THOMAS WYLIE

authorHOUSE®

AuthorHouse™
1663 Liberty Drive
Bloomington, IN 47403
www.authorhouse.com
Phone: 1 (800) 839-8640

Published by AuthorHouse 04/07/2020

ISBN: 978-1-7283-5830-7 (sc)
ISBN: 978-1-7283-5829-1 (e)

Print information available on the last page.

This book is printed on acid-free paper.

Contents

AMBITION

ANGER

BEAUTY

BITTERNESS

BOREDOM

CELEBRATION

CHANGE

CHEATING

CHRISTLIKENESS

COMFORT

COMPASSION

COMPETITION

COMPLACENCY

COMPLAINING

COMPROMISE

CONFIDENCE

CONFESSION

CONFLICT

CONSEQUENCES

CONTENTMENT

CONTROL

COOPERATION

COURAGE

CRITICISM

DEATH

DECEIT

DECISIONS

DEPRESSION

DESIRES

DIVORCE

ENCOURAGEMENT

ENVIRONMENT

EXAMPLE

EXCELLENCE

FAILURE

FAITH

FAITHFULNESS

FAMILY

FEAR

FORGIVENESS

FRIENDSHIP

FRUSTRATION

GIVING

GOODNESS

GOSSIP

GRACE

GREED

GRIEF

GUILT

HABITS

HAPPINESS

HATRED

HEALING

HELP

HONESTY

HOPE

HOSPITALITY

HUMILITY

INSIGNIFICANCE

INTIMACY

JEALOUSY

JUSTICE

KINDNESS

LEADERSHIP

LISTENING

LONELINESS

LOSS

LOVE

LOYALTY

Introduction

SOME OF THE TIME it is elusive solutions (hard to find answers) to life's issues when we need them the most. "Promises From God's Word, (Book I)" is an assortment of promises from God's Word (The Bible) which are spiritual, inspirational, motivational, devotional which are designed as an important instrument for finding what God has to say about our specific needs or circumstances. Each topic throughout this publication is listed in alphabetical order from "A" through "L." Every section contains interesting inquiries regarding the matter, answers from Scripture (with references), and a promise from God's Word (Authorized King James Translation unless otherwise indicated).

It is the author's expectation that this reading and hope makes the Bible open, helpful, and accessible for all who reference its pages.

ACCEPTANCE

1. How do we learn to accept those who are different from us?

"And it came to pass, as Jesus sat at meat in the house, behold, many publicans and sinners came and sat down with him and his disciples." "And when the Pharisees saw it, they said unto his disciples, Why eateth your Master with publicans and sinners?" "But when Jesus heard that, he said unto them, They that be whole need not a physician, but they that are sick."

(Matthew 9:10-12 KJV)

Accepting others may require us to take a look at individuals from an alternate point of view.

2. What if a person has committed a terrible sin? Do we still accept him or her?

"For I am persuaded, that neither death, nor life, nor angels, nor principalities, nor powers, nor things present, nor things to come," "Nor height, nor depth, nor any other creature, shall be able to separate us from the love of God, which is in Christ Jesus our Lord."

(Romans 8:38-39 KJV)

Nothing we do can separate us from God's love. Similarly, we ought to consistently love others. This doesn't mean we acknowledge or approve their corrupt (sinful) activities, yet we love and acknowledge them as one of a kind and unique creations of God.

3. Are there times we should not be accepting?

"For in the eighth year of his reign, while he was yet young, he began to seek after the God of David his father: and in the twelfth year he began to purge Judah and Jerusalem from the high places, and the groves, and the carved images, and the molten images." And they brake down the altars of Ba'-al-im in his presence; and the images, that were on high above them, he cut down; and the groves, and the carved images, be brake in pieces, and made dust of them, and strowed it upon the graves of them that had sacrificed unto them."

And he burnt the bones of the priests upon their altars, and cleansed Judah and Jerusalem." "And so did he in the cities of Ma-mas'-seh, and E'-phra-im, and

Simeon, even unto Naph'-ta-li, with their mattocks round about."

"And when he had broken down altars and the groves, and had beaten the graven images into powder, and cut down all the idols throughout all the land of Israel, he returned to Jerusalem."

(II Chronicles 34: 3-7 RSV)

What this Scripture is stating is: we should not accept or endure (tolerate) sin in our own lives. Sin is our foe, trying to wreck us. If we permit a particular sin to abide in our heart unattended, it will start to spread like a dangerous tumor, (similar to a malignant cancer) influencing all we think and do.

PROMISE FROM GOD

"Wherefore receive ye one another, as Christ also received us to the glory of God." In other words, accept each other just as Jesus Christ has accepted you; then God will be glorified.

ACCOUNTABILITY

4. How do I become more accountable?

"Blessed is the man that walketh not in the counsel of the ungodly, nor standeth in the way of sinners, nor sitteth in the way of sinners, nor sitteth in the seat of the scornful."

(Psalm 1:1 ASV)

"Faithful are the wounds of a friend; but the kisses of an enemy are deceitful."

(Proverbs 27:6 KJV)

To turn out to be progressively responsible, follow God's commands as illustrated in his Word, the Bible, And pick savvy (wise) companions to whom you can don't hesitate to give a record of yourself.

"The way of a fool is right in his own eyes: but he that hearkeneth unto counsel is wise." (Proverbs 12:15 KJV). Good advisers keep us from actions or sins that can hurt us.

5. How can we choose people to hold us accountable?

“But he forsook the counsel of the old men, which they had given him, and consulted with the young men that were grown up with him, and which stood before him:” “And he said unto them, What counsel give ye that we may answer this people, who have spoken to me, saying, Make the yoke which thy father did put upon us lighter?”

And the young men that were grown up with him spake unto him, saying Thus shalt thou speak unto this people that spake unto thee, saying, Thy father made our yoke heavy, but make thou it lighter unto us; thus shalt thou say unto them, My little finger shall be thicker than my father's loins.” And now whereas my father did lade you with heavy yoke, I will add to your yoke: my father hath chastised you with ships, but I will chastise you with scorpions.”

(I Kings12:8-11 KJV)

Rehoboam: “(Let them know) If you think he was difficult for you, simply keep a watch out what I'll be like!...”

Friends are not always the best counselors, particularly if their guidance or counsel isn't steady (consistent) with God's Word.

6. How can I effectively hold someone else accountable?

"Moreover thou shalt provide out of all the people able men, such as fear God, men of truth, hating covetousness; and place such over them to be rulers of thousands, and rulers of hundreds, rulers of fifties, and rulers of tens:" And let them judge the people at all seasons: and it shall be, that every great matter they shall bring unto thee, but every small matter they shall judge: so shall it be easier for thyself, and they shall bear the burden with thee." If thou shalt do this thing, and God command thee so, then thou shalt be able to endure, and all this people shall also go to their place in peace." "So Moses hearkened to the voice of his father in law, and did all that he had said."

(Exodus 18:21-24 KJV)

"If any be blameless, the husband of one wife, having faithful children not accused of riot or unruly." For a bishop must be blameless, as a steward of God; not self-willed, not soon angry, not given to wine, no striker, not given to filthy lucre;" But a lover of hospitality, a lover of good men, sober, just, holy, temperate;"

"Holding fast the faithful word as he hath been taught, that he may be able by sound doctrine both to exhort and to convince the gainsayers."

(Titus 1:6-9 KJV)

In the event that we are going to minister to others by holding them accountable, we should be insightful (wise), legitimate (honest), faithful, godly and trustworthy.

7. Does God really hold us accountable for all our actions?

"Rejoice, O young man, in thy youth; and let thy heart cheer thee in the days of thy youth, and walk in the ways of thine heart, and in the sight of thine eyes: but know thou that for all these things God will bring thee into judgment."

(Ecclesiastes 11:9 KJV)

Appreciate, enjoy life, however remain inside God's commands. God will hold us accountable for all that we do, and who needs to disclose corruption or ungodly living to a Holy God upon the arrival of judgment?

"Can any hid himself in secret places that I shall not see him? Saith the LORD. Do not I fill heaven and earth? Saith the LORD."

(Jeremiah 23:24 KJV)

What you retain from another regularly blasts into full view sometime in the not too distant future. So why not look for counsel now? In addition, God knows every one of the insider facts (secrets) in your heart.

PROMISE FROM GOD

"Wherewithal shall a young man cleanse his way? By taking heed thereto according to thy word." "Teach me good judgment and knowledge: for I have believed thy commandments."

(Psalm 119:9, 66 KJV)

In what capacity can a youngster remain pure? By complying with your promise and following its commands...now show me trustworthiness (good judgment) and knowledge.

AMBITION

8. When is ambition good?

"And that ye study to be quiet, and to do your own business, and to work with your own hands, as we commanded you; That ye may walk honestly toward them that are without, and that ye may have lack of nothing."

(I Thessalonians 4:11, 12 KJV)

"Yea, so have I strived to preach the gospel, not where Christ was named, lest I should build upon another man's foundation:"

(Romans 15:20 KJV)

Ambition is good when it is directed not at the size of an accomplishment but at the quality of our character. Paul ambition was to preach the Good News where the name of Christ has never been heard. Paul's ambition was to preach about Christ around the world.

9. When does ambition become destructive or sinful?

"And the whole earth was of one language, and of one speech." "And it came to pass, as they journeyed from the east, that they found a plain in the land of Shi'-nar; and they dwelt there." "And another said one to another, Go to, let us make brick for stone, and slime had they for morter." "And they said, Go to, let us build as a city and a tower, whose top may reach unto heaven; and let us make as a name, lest we be scattered abroad upon the face of the whole earth."

(Genesis 11:1-4 KJV)

Again, the devil taketh him up into an exceeding high mountain, and sheweth him all the kingdoms of the world, and the glory of them;" "And saith unto him, All these things will I give thee, if thou will fall down and worship me." Then saith Jesus unto him, Get thee hence, Satan: for it is written, THOU SHALT WORSHIP THE LORD THY GOD, AND HIM ONLY SHALT THOU SERVE."

(Matthew 4:8-10 KJV)

"And James and John, the sons of Zeb'-e-dee, come unto him, saying, Master, we would that thou shouldest do for us whatsoever we shall desire." "And he said unto them, What would ye that I should do for you?"

"They said unto him, Grant unto us that we may sit, one on thy right hand, and the other on thy left hand, in thy glory."

"But Jesus said unto them, Ye know not what ye ask: Can ye drink of the cup that I drink of? And be baptized with the baptism that I am baptized with?" "And they said unto him, We can. And Jesus said unto them, Ye shall indeed drink of the cup that I drink of; and with the baptism that I am baptized withal shall ye be baptized:"

"But to sit on my right hand and on my left hand is not mine to give; but it shall be given to them for whom it is prepared." And when the ten heard it, they began to be much displeased with James and John." But Jesus called them to him, and saith unto them, Ye know that they which are accounted to rule over the Gentiles exercise lordship over them; and their great ones exercise authority upon them." But so shall it not be among you: but whosoever will be great among you, shall be your minister:" "And whosoever of will be the chiefest, shall be servant of all." "For even the

Son of man came not to be ministered unto, but to minister, and to give his life a ransom for many."

(Mark 10:35-45 KJV)

Ambition can turn into that which Satan uses to bait us away from God and toward obliteration. Childish aspiration (Selfish ambition) can even curve our companionships (friendships) and discipleship into insignificant spiritual competitiveness.

10. How can we use ambition to glorify God?

"Let nothing be done through strife or vainglory; but in lowliness of mind let each esteem other better than themselves."

(Philippians 2:3 KJV)

Selfish ambition turns out to be authentic when changed (transformed) by an individual relationship with Jesus Christ.

Promise From God (Psalm 119:1-5) Happy are individuals of trustworthiness, who adhere to the law of the LORD. Happy are those who..search for him with their entire being..

ANGER

11. What are the effects of anger?

“And Esau hated Jacob because of the blessing wherewith his father blessed him: and Esau said in his heart, The days of mourning for my father are at hand; then will I slay my brother Jacob.”

“And these words of Esau her elder son were told to Rebekah: and she sent and called Jacob her younger son, and said unto him, Behold, thy brother Esau, as touching thee, doth comfort himself, purposing to kill thee.” “Now therefore, my son, obey my voice; and arise, flee thou to Laban my brother to Ha’-ran...”

(Genesis 27:41-43 KJV)

Anger separates us from others (Isolates)

“Cease from anger, and forsake wrath: fret not thyself in any wise to do evil.”

(Psalm 37:8 KJV)

Stop your anger!...Do not begrudge others - it just prompts hurt (it leads to harm)

"Wherefore, my beloved brethren, let every man be swift to hear, slow to speak, slow to wrath:" "Doe the wrath of man worketh not the righteousness of God."

(James 1:19, 20 KJV)

Anger can not make things right in God's sight. Anger produces ungodliness and evil emotions in us.

"Then Saul's anger was kindled against Jonathan, and he said unto him, Thou son of the perverse rebellious woman, do not I know that thou hast chosen the son of Jessee to thine own confusion, and unto the confusion of thy mother's nakedness?" "For as long as the son of Jesse liveth upon the ground, thou shalt not be established, nor thy kingdom. Wherefore now send and fetch him unto me, for he shall surely die."

(I Samuel 20:30,31KJV)

Anger (outrage) blinds us to what is great and right. Saul's envious indignation blinded him to the way that God had already chosen David to be the following king as a result of his faithful character.

"And Adam knew Eve his wife; and she conceived, and bare Cain, and said, I have gotten a man from the LORD."

"And she again bare his brother Abel. And Abel was a keeper of sheep, but Cain was a tiller of the ground."

"And in process of time it came to pass, that Cain brought of the fruit of the ground an offering unto the LORD."

"And Abel, he also brought of the firstlings of his flock and of the fat thereof. And the LORD had respect unto Abel and to his offering;"

"But unto Cain and to his offering he had not respect. And Cain was very wroth, and his countenance fell."

And the LORD said unto Cain, Why art thou wroth? And why is thy countenance fallen?"

If thou doest well, shalt thou not be accepted? And if thou doest not well, sin lieth at the door. And unto thee shall be his desire, and thou shalt rule over him."

"And Cain talked with Abel his brother; and it came to pass, when they were in the field, that Cain rose up against Abel his brother, and slew him."

"And the LORD said unto Cain, Where is Abel thy brother? And he said, I know not; Am I my brother's keeper?"

"And he said, What hast thou done? The voice of thy brother's blood crieth unto me from the ground."

And now art thou cursed from the earth, which hath opened her mouth to receive thy brother's blood from thy hand;" "When thou tillest the ground, it shall not henceforth yield unto thee her strength; a fugitive and a vagabond shalt thou be in the earth."*This tells us that anger in its strongest form can lead to murder.

(Genesis 4:1-12 KJV)

"A SOFT answer turneth away wrath; but grievous words stir up anger."

(Proverbs 15:1 KJV)

A delicate (gentle) answer dismisses fierceness (anger), yet brutal (harsh) words work up to outrage, anger. Anger prompts struggle and contentions (conflict and arguments).

12. When we are angry, what should we avoid?

"But if any caused grief, he hath not grieved me, but in part: that I may not overcharge you all."

"Sufficient to such a man is this punishment, which was inflicted of many."

"So that contrariwise ye ought rather to forgive him, and comfort him, lest perhaps such a one should be swallowed up with overmuch sorrow."

"Wherefore I beseech you that ye would confirm your love toward him."

(II Corinthians 2:5-8 KJV)

"And, ye fathers, provoke not your children to wrath; but bring them up in the nurture and admonition of the Lord."

(Ephesians 6:4 KJV)

"Even so the tongue is a fire, a world of iniquity; so is the tongue among our members, that it defileth the whole body, and setteth on fire the course of nature; and it is set on fire of hell."

(James 3:5 KJV)

The tongue is a small thing, but what great damage it can do.

"And the evil spirit from the LORD was upon Saul, as he sat in his house with his javelin in his hand: and David played with his hand." And Saul sought to smite David even to the wall with the javelin; but he slipped away out of Saul's presence, and he smote the javelin into the wall: and David fled, and escaped that night."

Abstain from expressing your real thoughts when you are angry. You will undoubtedly say something you will regret. Abstain from following up on motivation in the heat of anger. You will undoubtedly accomplish something you will regret.

13. We all get angry sometimes, so what should we do about it?

"BE YE ANGRY, AND SIN NOT; let not the sun go down upon your wrath:"

"Neither give place to the devil"

(Ephesians 4:26)

Try not to let anger assume control for you. Try not to release the sun down while you are as yet furious, for anger gives a relentless a dependable balance (foothold) to the Devil.

Anger resembles a skunk in the house. Try not to bolster it to urge it to remain. What's more, attempt to dispose of it as quickly as time permits.

"Ye have heard that it was said by them of old time, THOU SHALT NOT KILL; and whosoever shall kill shall be in danger of the judgment:" But I say unto you, That whosoever is angry with his brother without a cause shall be in danger of the judgment; and whosoever shall say to his brother, Ra'ca, shall be in danger of the council: but whosoever shall say, Thou fool, shall be in danger of hell fire."

Therefore if thou bring thy gift to the altar, and there rememberest that thy brother hath ought against thee; Leave there thy gift before the altar, and go thy way; first be reconciled to thy brother, and then come and offer thy gift." "Agree with thine adversary quickly, whiles thou art in the way with him; lest at any time the adversary deliver thee to the judge, and the judge deliver thee to the officer, and thou be cast into prison."

"Verily I say unto thee, Thou shalt by no means come out thence, till thou hast paid the uttermost farthing."

(Matthew 5:21-26)

Face those with whom you are irate so as to reestablish your relationship.

"Doth not behave itself unseemly, seeketh not her own, is not easily provoked, thinketh no evil;..."

(I Corinthians 13:5)

Love is the mightiest weapon in overcoming anger.

PROMISE FROM GOD

"The LORD is merciful and gracious, slow to anger, and plenteous in mercy." (The LORD is full of unfailing Love)

(Psalm 103:8)

BEAUTY

14. Who is a beautiful person in God's eyes?

"But the LORD said unto Samuel, Look not on his countenance, or on the height of his stature; because I have refused him: for the LORD seeth not as man seeth; for man looketh on the outward appearance, but the LORD looketh on the heart."

(I Samuel 16:7)

We train our eyes to take a look at somebody's physical appearance. God sees through physical appearance into the heart. Society time and again accepts that a ugly face with a delightful (beautiful) heart is an ugly person. To God, real beauty originates from what our identity is, not what we resemble.

15. Beauty may be a blessing, but how can it harm or corrupt us?

"On the seventh day, when the heart of the king was merry with wine, he commanded Me-hu'-man, Biz'-tha, Har-bo'-na, Big'-tha, and A-bag'-tha, Ze'-thar, and Car'-cas, the seven chamberlains that served in the presence of A-has-u-e'-rus the king,"

"To bring Vash'-ti the queen before the king with the crown royal, to shew the people and the princes her beauty: for she was fair to look on."

"But the queen Vash'-ti refused to come at the king's commandment by his chanberlains: therefore was the king very wroth, and his anger burned in him."

"Then the king said to the wise men, which knew the times, (for so was the king's manner toward all that knew the law and judgment;"

"And the next unto him was Car-she'-na, She'-thar, Ad-ma'-tha, Tar'-shish, Me'-res, Mar'-se-na, and Me-mu-can, the seven princes of Persia and Me'-di-a, which saw the king's face, and which sat the first in the kingdom;)"

"What shall we do unto the queen Vash'-ti according to law, because she hath not performed the commandment of the king A-has-u-e'-rus by the chamberlains?"

"And Me-mu'-can answered before the king and the princes; Vash'-ti the queen hath not done wrong to the king only, but also to all the princes, and to all the people that are in the provinces of the king A-has-u-e'rus."

"For this deed of the queen shall come abroad unto all women, so that they shall despise their husbands in their eyes, when it shall be reported, The king A-has-u-e'-rus commanded Vash'-ti the queen to be brought in before him, but she came not."

"Likewise shall the ladies of Persia and Me'-di-a say this day unto all the king's princes, which have heard of the deed of the queen. Thus shall arise too much contempt and wrath."

"If it please the king, let there go a royal commandment from him, and let it be written among the laws of the Persians and the Medes, that it be not altered, That Vash'-ti come no more3 before king A-has-u-e-rus;

and let the king give her royal estate unto another that is better than she."

"And when the king's decree which he shall make shall be published throughout all his empire, (for It is great,) all the wives shall give to their husbands honour, both to great and small."

(Esther 1:10-20)

"Thine heart was lifted up because of thy beauty, thou hast corrupted thy wisdom by reason of thy brightness: I will cast thou to the ground, I will lay thee before kings, that they may behold thee."

(Ezekiel 28:17)

Since we will in general have a misinformed perspective (misguided view) on beauty, the individuals who are truly beautiful can be hurt by it. They can likewise use their beauty in a degenerate manner (corruptible way). Furthermore, the individuals who are not so beautiful may become victims of discrimination.

"And tookest thy broidered garments, and coverest them: and thou hast set mine oil and mine incense before them."

"Thou hast built thy high place at every head of the way, and hast made thy beauty to be abhorred, and hast opened thy feet to every one that passed by, and multiplied thy whoredoms."

(Ezekiel 16:18, 25)

You used the beautifully weaved garments I offered you to cover your idol images. At that point you used my oil and incense to worship them...you polluted (defiled) your beauty, offering your body to each bystander in a perpetual stream of prostitution.

Beauty can be used for underhandedness (evil purposes), and when it is, it becomes something terrible, something very ugly.

16. Is inward beauty more important than outward beauty?

"Whose adorning let it not be that outward adorning of plaiting the hair, and of wearing of gold, or of putting on of apparel;"

"But let it be the hidden man of the heart, in that which is not corruptible, even the ornament of a meek and quiet spirit, which is in the sight of God of great price."

"For after this manner in the old time the holy women also, who trusted in God, adorned themselves, being in subjection unto their own husbands:"

(I Peter 3:3-5 KJV)

Physical beauty blurs (fades) with age. Internal beauty can mature with age. While we as a whole value looking as pleasant as possible, and endeavor to do as such, it is that inward beauty that wins, presently and over the long haul.

PROMISE FROM GOD

Favour is deceitful, and beauty is vain; but a woman that feareth the LORD, she shall be praised."

(Proverbs 31:30 KJV)

Charm is beguiling (deceptive), and beauty doesn't last; yet a woman who fears the Lord will be greatly praised.

BITTERNESS

17. How do we become bitter?

"And Esau hated Jacob because of the blessing wherewith his father blessed him: and Esau said in his heart, The days of mourning for my father are at hand; then will I slay my brother Jacob."

Esau hated Jacob because he had stolen his blessing.

(Genesis 27:41 KJV)

"And went Ha'-man forth that day joyful and with a glad heart; but when Ha'-man saw Mor'-de-cai in the king's gate, that he stood not up, nor moved for him, he was full of indignation against mor-de-cai."

(Esther 5:9 KJV)

What a cheerful (joyful) man Haman was as he left the meal (banquet)! In any case, when he saw Mordecai sitting at the entryway, not standing up or trembling apprehensively before him, he was angry.

We frequently become bitter by letting outrage (anger) and disdain (hatred) control us.

"Let all bitterness, and wrath, and anger, and clamour, and evil speaking, be put away from you, with all malice:"

And be ye kind to another, tenderhearted, forgiving one another, even as God for Christ's sake hath forgiven you."

We frequently become bitter when we demand our way and quit pardoning (forgiving) and forgetting. We would do well to recall that God has forgiven us in spite of our consistent wicked inclinations (sinful ways).

(Ephesians 4:31, 32 RSV)

"Looking diligently lest any man fail of the grace of God; lest any root of bitterness springing up trouble you, and thereby many be defiled;..."

Watch our that no bitter base of unbelief ascends among you, for at whatever point it jumps up, many are defiled by its toxin.

We become unpleasant or bitter by overlooking God's grace, which is showered upon us every day.

(Hebrews 12:15)

18. How can we cause bitterness in others?

"ye who turn judgment to wormwood, and leave off righteousness in the earth,"

You wicked people! You wind (twist) justice, making it a harsh pill for poor people and mistreated (oppressed). Honesty and reasonable play are good for nothing fictions to you.

We can cause bitterness in others when we are shameful or unreasonable in our dealings with others, especially the individuals who are poor and abused (oppressed).

(Amos 5:7 KJV)

19. What remedy is there for bitterness?

"So that contrariwise ye ought rather to forgive him, and comfort him, lest perhaps such a one should be swallowed up with overmuch sorrow."

There are times when straightforward absolution (SIMPLE FORGIVENESS) can mitigate a lifetime of harshness (bitterness). Recuperation from intense bitterness might be as unpredictable as the purposes behind the harshness, however it might likewise be as straightforward as three expressed words: "I FORGIVE YOU."

(II Corinthians 2:7 KJV)

PROMISE FROM GOD

"Thou wilt keep him in perfect peace, whose mind is stayed on thee; because he trusteth in thee." "Or let him take hold of my strength, that he may make peace with me; and he shall make peace with me."

You will keep in flawless harmony (perfect peace) all who trust in you, whose musings (thoughts) are fixed on you!

(Isaiah 26:3; 27:5 KJV)

BOREDOM

20. Doesn't being a Christian sound boring to non-Christians (unbelievers)?

"That ye be not slothful, but followers of them who through faith and patience inherit the promises."

That you won't become spiritually dull and uninterested. Be that as it may, that you will follow the case of the individuals who will inherit God's promises due to their faith and persistence (patience).

Concentrating (focusing) on the everlasting rewards God vows to adherents should make life persistently energizing. In the event that we become exhausted in our Christian life it is on the grounds that we are not walking with God and experiencing the day by day blessings he is prepared to give us.

(Hebrews 6:12 KJV)

21. How do I keep faithfulness in marriage from being boring?

"Let thy fountain be blessed: and rejoice with the wife of thy youth."

"Let her be as loving hind and pleasant roe; let her beasts satisfy thee at all times; and be thou ravished always with her love"

God doesn't expect or intend faithfulness in a union of marriage to be boring. Genuine happiness comes when we commit ourselves in discovering joy in the relationship God has given us.

(Proverbs 5:18, 19 KJV)

22. Is not a life of sin more exciting?

"The backslider in heart shall be filled with his own ways: and a good man shall be satisfied from himself."

The sinful backslider gets what he merits (what he deserves); good people get their reward.

With God it is difficult to get bored, for his reach is as wide (board) as the universe and as far as eternity.

(Proverbs 14:14 KJV)

"Go and cry in the ears of Jerusalem, saying, Thus saith the LORD; I remember thee, the kindness of thy youth, the love of thine espousals, when thou wentest after me in the wilderness, in a land that was not sown."

For what reason do you will not abandon such an excess of pursuing different idol beings (other gods)? Pursuing different other gods (idols) is a tiring business, one interest after another closures with frustration and disappointment. Sin has a weakening equivalence at its core. It is just dress that changes. God alone really fulfills. God alone fully satisfies.

(Jeremiah 2:2 KJV)

PROMISE FROM GOD

"And let us not be weary in well doing; for in due season we shall reap, if we faint not."

So don't become weary of doing what is right. Try not to get discouraged and surrender, for we will reap a harvest of blessing at the proper time.

(Galatians 6:9 KJV)

CELEBRATION

23. Does God want us to celebrate?

"Seven weeks shalt thou number unto thee: begin to number the seven weeks from such time as thou beginest to put the sickle to the corn."

"And thou shalt keep the feast of weeks unto the LORD thy God with a tribute of a freewill offering of thine hand, which thou shalt give unto the LORD thy God, according as the LORD thy God hath blessed thee:"

"And thou shalt rejoice before the LORD thy God, thou, and thy son, and thy daughter, and thy man-servant, and thy maidservant, and the Levite that is within thy gates, and the stranger, and the fatherless, and the widow, that are among you, in the place which the LORD thy God hath chosen to place his name there."

"And thou shalt remember that thou wast a bondsman in Egypt; and thou shalt observe and do these statutes."

Thou shalt observe the feast of tabernacles seven days, after that thou hast gathered in thy corn and thy wine:"

"And thou shalt rejoice in thy feast, thou, and thy son, and thy daughter, and thy manservant, and thy maidservant, and the Levite, the stranger, and the fatherless, and the widow, that are within thy gates."

Seven days shalt thou keep a solemn feast unto the LORD thy God in the place which the LORD shall choose: because the LORD thy God shall bless thee in all thine increase, and in all the works of thine hands, therefore thou shalt surely rejoice."

"Three times in a year shall all thy males appear before the LORD thy God in the place which he shall choose; in the feast of unleavened bread, and in the feast of tabernacles: and they shall not appear before the LORD empty:"

"Every man shall give as he is able, according to the blessing of the LORD thy God which he hath given thee."

We celebrate to express gratitude toward God for all he has accomplished for us, to review his acts of goodness, and to appreciate each other's company.

(Deuteronomy 16:9-17 KJV)

"Then he said unto them, Go your way, eat the fat, and drink the sweet, and send portions unto them for whom nothing is prepared: for this day is holy unto our Lord: neither be ye sorry; for the joy of the LORD is your strength."

Joy and fun, as God intended, are significant pieces of festivity since they lift our spirits and assist us with seeing the beauty and importance (meaning) throughout everyday life.

(Nehemiah 8:10 KJV)

"Ye shall do no servile work therein: but ye shall offer an offering made by fire unto the LORD."

Celebration allows us to rest and focus on what is good. It should take our minds off the ordinary and routine.

(Leviticus 23:25 KJV)

"This day came ye out in the month A'-bib.

"And it shall be when the LORDshall bring thee into the land of the Ca'-naan-ites, and Hit'-tites, and the Am'-or-ites, and the Hi'-vites, and the Jeb'-u-sites, which he sware unto thy fathers to give thee, a land flowing with milk and honey, that thou shalt keep this service in this month."

"Seven days thou shalt eat unleavened bread, and in the seventh day shall be a feast to the LORD."

"Unleavened bread shall be eaten seven days; and there shall no leavened bread be seen with thee, neither shall be leaven seen with thee in all thy quarters."

'And thou shalt shew thy son in that day, saying, This is done because of that which the LORD did unto me when I came forth out of Egypt."

"And it shall be for a sign unto thee upon thine hand, and for a memorial between thine eyes, that the

LORD'S law may be in thy mouth: for with a strong hand hath the LORD brought thee out of Egypt."

"Thou shalt therefore keep this ordinance in his season from year to year."

"And it shall be when the LORD shall bring thee into the land of the Ca'-naan-ites, as he sware unto thee and to thy fathers, and shall give it thee."

We celebrate to mark significant achievements in our lives; we likewise celebrate to show our youngsters a definitive explanation behind our festival.

(Exodus 13:4-11 KJV)

"O CLAP your hands, all ye people; shout unto God with the voice of triumph."

(Psalm 47:1 KJV)

"Make a joyful noise unto the LORD, all the earth: make a loud noise, and rejoice, and sing praise."

(Psalm 98:4-6 KJV)

"PRAISE ye the LORD. Praise God in his sanctuary: praise him in the firmament of his power."

"Praise him for his mighty acts: praise him according to his excellent greatness."

"Praise him with the sound of the trumpet: praise him with the psaltery and harp."

"Praise him with the timbrel and dance: praise him with stringed instruments and organs."

"Praise him upon the loud cymbals: praise him upon the loud cymbals: praise him upon the high sounding cymbals."

Let every thing that hath breath praise the LORD. Praise ye the LORD."

We celebrate to praise and love God since he loves us, due to the blessing he has given us on earth, and due to the eternal blessings he has waiting for us in heaven.

(Psalm 150:1-6 KJV)

24. Which celebrations are inappropriate?

"And when Moses saw that the people were naked; (for Aaron had made them naked unto their shame among their enemies:)"

At the point when Moses saw that Aaron had let the individuals get totally crazy (out of control) - and a lot to the delight of their enemies....

(Exodus 32:25 KJV)

"AND Israel abode in Shit'-tim, and the people began to commit whoredom with the daughters of Moab."

"And they called the people unto the sacrifices of their gods: and the people did eat, and bowed down to their gods."

(Numbers 25:1, 2 KJV)

"For the time past of our life may suffice us to have wrought the will of the Gentiles, when we walked in lasciviousness, banquetings, and abominable idolatries:"

Celebration that is conceited (self-centered), liberal, includes wicked acts, sinful acts or has conditions that can entice you into sin isn't right.

(I Peter 4:3 KJV)

25. As far as celebration goes, are there not times when God alone should be the focus?

"For the LORD thy God hath blessed thee in all the works of thy hand: he knoweth thy walking through this great wilderness: these forty years the LORD thy God hath been with thee; thou hast lacked nothing."

Through life's journey and its customary achievements, God has been there to supply all we need.

Celebration ought to be a period for the sake of entertainment and eating, obviously, yet it ought to likewise be a period for thanksgiving to God for his blessings to us.

Praise events, commend people, however the greater part of all, celebrate God.

(Deuteronomy 2:7 KJV)

PROMISE FROM GOD

"But let All those that put their trust in thee rejoice: let them ever shout for joy, because thou defendest them: Let them also that love thy name be joyful in thee."

(Psalm 5:11 KJV)

CHANGE

26. With all the change in my life, how can the Bible help me keep it all together?

"Because of his strength will I wait upon thee: for God is my defence."

"The God of my mercy shall prevent me: God shall let me see my desire upon mine enemies."

(Psalm 59:9, 10 KJV)

"AND AS A VESTURE SHALT THOU FOLD THEM UP, AND THEY SHALL, BE CHANGED: BUT THOU ART THE SAME, AND THY YEARS SHALL NOT FAIL."

Be that as it may, you are consistently the same...We can confide in the character of God to be constant (unchanging) and solid (reliable).

(Hebrews 1:12 KJV)

"Jesus Christ the same yesterday, and to day, and for ever."

We can place our faith in Jesus Christ, whose love and grace are eternal.

(Hebrews 13:8 RSV)

"Heaven and earth shall pass away: but my words shall not pass away."

We can build our lives on God's Word because its truth is changeless.

(Mark 13:31 KJV)

"And we know that all things work together for good to them that love God, to them who are the called according to his purpose."

God can work his will even through traumatic, flighty, and unjustifiable change.

(Romans 8:28 KJV)

27. I Know there are things in my life I should change, but how?

"And Saul, yet breathing out threatenings and slaughter against the disciples of the Lord, went unto the high priest,"

"And desired of him letters to Damascus to the synagogues, that if he found any of this way, whether they were men or women, he might bring them bound unto Jerusalem."

"And as he journeyed, he came near Damascus: and suddenly there shined round about him a light from heaven:"

"And he fell to the earth, and heard a voice saying unto him, Saul, Saul, why persecutest thou me?"

"And he said, Who art thou, Lord? And the Lord said, I am Jesus whom thou persecutest: it is hard for thee to kick against the pricks."

"And he trembling and astonished said, Lord, what wilt thou have me to do? And the Lord said unto him, Arise, and go into the city, and it shall be told thee what thou must do."

"And the men which journeyed with him stood speechless, hearing a voice, but seeing no man."

"And Saul arose from the earth; and when his eyes were opened, he saw no man: but they led him by the hand, and brought him into Damascus."

"And he was three days without sight, and neither did eat nor drink."

"And there was a certain disciple at Damascus, named An-a-ni'-as and to him said the Lord in a vision, An-a-ni'-as. And he said, Behold, I am here, Lord."

"Ande the Lord said unto him, Arise, and go into the street which is called Straight, and enquire in the house of Judas for one called Saul, of Tar'-sus; for, behold, he prayeth,"

"And hath seen in a vision a man named An-a-ni'-as coming in, and putting his hand on him, that he might receive his sight."

"Then An-a-ni'-as answered, Lord, I have heard by many of this man, how much evil he hath done to thy saints at Jerusalem:"

"And here he hath authority from the chief priests to bind all that call on thy name."

"But the Lord said unto him, Go thy way: for he is a chosen vessel unto me, to bear my name before the Gentiles, and kings, and the children of Israel:"

"For I will shew him how great things he must suffer for my name's sake."

"And An-a-ni'-as went his way, and entered into the house; and putting his hands on him said, Brother Saul, the Lord, even Jesus, that appeared unto thee in the way as thou camest, hath sent me, that thou mightest receive thy sight, and be filled with the Holy Ghost."

"And immediately there fell from his eyes as it had been scales: and he received sight forthwith, and arose, and was baptized."

"And when he had received meat, he was strengthened. Then was Saul certain days with the disciples which were at Damascus."

"And straightway he preached Christ in the synagogues, that he is the Son of God."

But all that heard him were amazed, and said; Is not this he that destroyed them which called on this name in Jerusalem, and came hither for that intent, that he might bring them bound unto the chief priests?"

"But Saul increased the more in strength, and confounded the Jews which dwelt at Damascus, proving that this is very Christ.

Jesus comes as a divine, devout, personal (individual) experience (encounter) with Jesus Christ.

(Acts 9:1- 22 KJV)

"And Jesus entered and passed through Jericho."

"And, behold, there was a man named Zac-chae'us, which was the chief among the publicans, and he was rich."

"And he sought to see Jesus who he was; and could not for the press, because he was little of stature."

"And he ran before, and climbed up into a sycomore tree to see him: for he was to pass that way."

"And when Jesus came to the place, he looked up, and saw him, and said to him, Zac-chae'-us, make haste, and come down; for to day I must abide at thy house."

"And he made haste, and came down, and received him joyfully."

'And when they saw it, they all murmured, saying, That he was gone to be guest with a man that is a sinner."

"And Zac-chae'-us stood, and said unto the Lord; Behold, Lord, the half of my goods I give to the poor;

and if I have taken any thing from any man by false accusation, I restore him fourfold."

"And Jesus said unto him, This day is salvation come to this house, forsomuch as he also is a son of Abraham."

"For the Son of man is come to seek and to save that which was lost."

God calls us not only for a change of heart, but a change of behavior.

(Luke 19:1-10 KJV)

"Jesus went unto the mount of Olives."

"And early in the morning he came again into the temple, and all the people came unto him; and he sat down, and taught them."

"And the scribes and Pharisees brought unto him a woman taken in adultery; and when they had set her in the midst,"

"They say unto him, Master, this woman was taken in adultery, in the very act."

"Now Moses in the law commanded us, that such should be stoned; but what sayest thou?"

"This they said, tempting him, that they might have to accuse him. But Jesus stooped down, and with his finger wrote on the ground, as though he heard them not."

"So when they continued asking him, he lifted up himself, and said unto them, He that is without sin among you, let him first cast a stone at her."

"And again he stooped down, and wrote on the ground."

"And they which heard it, being convicted by their own conscience, went out one by one, beginning at the eldest, even unto the last: and Jesus was left alone, and the woman standing in the midst."

"When Jesus had lifted up himself, and saw none but the woman, he said unto her, Woman, where are those thine accusers? Hath no man condemned thee?"

"She said, No man, Lord. And Jesus said unto her, Neither do I condemn thee; go, and sin no more."

We don't change so as to get God's endorsement (approval), we change as a response to God's love.

(John 8:1-11 KJV)

"And he began to teach by the sea side; and there was gathered unto him a great multitude, so that he entered into a ship, and sat in the sea; and the whole multitude was by the sea on the land."

"And he taught them many things by parables, and said unto them in his doctrine,"

"Hearken; Behold, there went out a sower to sow:"

"And it came to pass, as he sowed, some fell by the way side, and the fowls of the air came and devoured it up."

'And some fell on stony ground, where it had not much earth; and immediately it sprang up, because it had no depth of earth:"

"But when the sun was up, it was scorched; and because it had no root, it withered away."

"And some fell among thorns, and the thorns grew up, and choked it, and it yielded no fruit."

'And other fell on good ground and did yield fruit that sprang up and increased; and brought forth, some thirty, some sixty, and some an hundred."

"And he said unto them, He that hath ears to hear, let him hear."

"And when he was alone, they that were about him with the twelve asked of him the parable."

And he said unto them, Unto you it is given to know the mystery of the kingdom of God; but unto them that are without, all these things are done in parables:"

"That SEEING THEY MAY SEE, AND NOT PERCEIVE; AND HEARING THEY MAY HEAR, AND NOT UNDERSTAND; LEST AT ANY TIME THEY SHOULD BE CONVERTED, AND THEIR SINS SHOULD BE FORGIVEN THEM."

"And he said unto them, Know ye not this parable? And how then will ye know all parables?"

"The sower soweth the word."

"And these are they by the way side, where the word is sown; but when they have heard, Satan cometh immediately, and taketh away the word that was sown in their hearts."

"And these are they likewise which are sown on stony ground; who, when they have heard the word, immediately receive it with gladness;"

"And have no root in themselves, and so endure but for a time; afterward, when affliction or persecution ariseth for the word's sake, immediately they are offended."

'And these are they which are sown among thorns; such as hear the word."

"And the cares of this world, and the deceitfulness of riches, and the lusts of other things entering in choke the word, and it becometh unfruitful."

"And these are they which are sown on good ground; such as hear the word, and receive it, and bring forth fruit, some thirtyfold, some sixty, and some an hundred."

Reality (truth) of God's promise produces change just when it is permitted to enter deep into our souls.

(Mark 4:1-20 KJV)

"And when Peter saw it, he answered unto the people, Ye men of Israel, why marvel ye at this? Or why look ye so earnestly on us, as though by our own power or holiness we had made this man to walk?"

"The God of Abraham, and of Isaac, and of Jacob, the God of our fathers, hath glorified his Son Jesus; whom ye delivered up, and denied him in the presence of Pilate, when he was determined to let him go."

"But ye denied the Holy One and the Just, and desired a murderer to be granted unto you;"

"And killed the Prince of life, whom God hath raised from the dead; whereof we are witnesses."

"And his name through faith in his name hath made this man strong, whom ye see and know; yea, the faith which is by him hath given him this perfect soundness in the presence of you all."

"And now, brethren, I wot that through ignorance ye did it, as did also your rulers."

"But those things, which God before had shewed by the mouth of all his prophets, that Christ should suffer, he hath so fulfilled."

"Repent ye therefore, and be converted, that your sins may be blotted out, when the times of refreshing shall come from the presence of the Lord;"

Here, change begins with truthful repentance.

(Acts 3:12-19 KJV)

PROMISE FROM GOD

"Therefore if any man be in Christ, he is a new creature: old things are passed away; behold, all things are become new."

This means the persons who become Christians become new people. They are not the equivalent (the same) any longer, for the old life is no more. A new life has started!

(II Corinthians 5:17 KJV)

CHEATING

28. What does God think of cheating? It is always wrong?

"A FALSE balance is abomination to the LORD: but a just weight is his delight."

The LORD detests (hates) cheating. However, He delights in trustworthiness (honesty). Cheating abuses (violates) a holy God. Cheating and faithfulness can't live respectively in harmony. One must yield to the next.

(Proverbs 11:1 KJV)

29. Is some cheating worse than other cheating?

“Which devour widows’ houses, and for a pretence make long prayers; these shall receive greater damnation.”

They boldly cheat widows out of their property; and afterward, to conceal the sort of individuals they truly are, they make long prayers in broad daylight.

Along these lines, their disciplines will be the more prominent.

Covering cheating with a devout glossing over is a twofold sin: first the wrongdoing of cheating and second the transgression of devout misdirection. God loathes both.

(Mark 12:40 KJV)

“He that is faithful in that which is least is faithful also in much: and he that is unjust in the least is unjust also in much.”

Except if you are faithful in little issues, you won't be faithful in huge ones. In the event that you cheat even a bit, you won't be straightforward with more noteworthy obligations.

Small cheating is removed of a similar bit of fabric as large cheating. Cheating will be cheating no (regardless of whether large or little).

(Luke 16:10 KJV)

PROMISE FROM GOD

'For this, THOU SHALT NOT COMMIT ADULTERY, THOU SHALT NOT KILL, THOU SHALT NOT STEAL, THOU SHALT NOT BEAR FALSE WITNESS, THOU SHALT NOT COVET; and if there be any other commandment, it is briefgly comprehended in this saying, namely, THOU SHALT LOVE THY NEIGHBOR AS THY SELF."

"Love worketh no ill to his neighbour: therefore love is the fulfilling of the law."

Love does no wrong to anybody, so love fulfills the entirety of God's requirements.

(Romans 13:9, 10 KJV)

CHRISTLIKENESS

30. How can we possibly even try to live like Jesus Christ?

"But ye are not in the flesh but in the Spirit, if so be that the Spirit of God dwell in you. Now if any man have not the Spirit of Christ, he is none of his."

(Romans 8:9 KJV)

"But of him are ye in Christ Jesus, Who of God is made unto us wisdom, and righteousness, and sanctification, and redemption:"

God alone made it possible for you to be in Christ Jesus. For our advantage (benefit) God made Christ to be wisdom itself. He is the one who made us worthy to God. He made us unadulterated (pure) and holy, and he offered himself t purchase our salvation.

By ourselves we can't hope to live like Christ, for we are not equipped (we just are not capable) of it. Yet, controlled by the Spirit of Christ in us, we can!

(I Corinthians 1:30 KJV)

31. How do we cultivate the Christlike spirit within us?

"But we all, with open face beholding as in a glass the glory of the Lord, are changed into the same image from glory to glory, even as by the Spirit of the Lord."

As we let Christ control our inward life, he additionally controls our external articulations of that internal life.

(II Corinthians 3:18 KJV)

"Unto the church of God which is at Corinth, to them that are sanctified in Christ Jesus, called to be saints, with all that in every place call upon the name of Jesus Christ our Lord, both their's and our's:"

"And such were some of you: but ye are washed, but ye are sanctified, but ye are justified in the name of the Lord Jesus, and by the Spirit of our God."

We are made more like Christ simply by believing in him.

(I Corinthians 1:2; 6:11 KJV)

"Sanctify them through thy truth; they word is truth."

We grow in Christlikeness by continually learning the truths of the Bible, and living by them.

(John 17:17 KJV)

"Having therefore these promises, dearly beloved, let us cleanse ourselves from all filthiness of the flesh and spirit, perfecting holiness in the fear of God."

Let us cleanse ourselves of everything that defiles our body or spirit. We become more Christlike by striving to keep sin out of our lives.

(II Corinthians 7:1 KJV)

"I BESEECH you therefore, brethren, by the mercies of God, that ye present your bodies a living sacrifice, holy, acceptable unto God, which is your reasonable service."

"And be not conformed to this world; but be ye transformed by the renewing of your mind, that ye may prove what is that good, and acceptable, and perfect, will of God."

How might we hope to be Christlike? All alone, it is beyond the realm of imagination, for we are corrupt, sinful individuals. In any case, we can give our bodies to God as an offering, a living sacrifice to him. He will help us with having Christlike conduct.

(Romans 12:1, 2 KJV)

"And hereby we do know him that we know him, if we keep his commandments."

What's more, how might we be certain that we belong to him? By glimpsing inside ourselves; would we say we are truly attempting to do what he needs us to?

This at that point turns into a test of our faith in Christ - would we say we are living as he needs, would we say we are carrying on with a Christlike life? If we are, it would propose that Christ lives inside. If we are not, it would suggest that he doesn't live inside.

(I John 2:3 KJV)

PROMISE FROM GOD

"Beloved, now are we the sons og God, and it doth not yet appear what we shall be; but we know that, when he shall appear, we shall be like him; for we shall see him as he is."

My brothers and sisters, we are as of now God's children, and we can't envision what we will resemble when Christ returns. Be that as it may, we do realize that when he comes we will be like him, for we will see him as he truly is (we shall see him as he is).

(I John 3:2 KJV)

COMFORT

32. When I am in trouble, where should I go first for comfort?

"I remembered thy judgments of old, O Lord; and have comforted myself."

(Psalm 119:52 KJV)

"Now our Lord Jesus Christ himself, and God, even our Father, which hath loved us, and hath given us everlasting consolation and good hope through grace,"

"Comfort your hearts, and stablish you in every good word and work."

Since God is our ultimate comfort, his Word is our most noteworthy resource for comfort. God's Word is as close as our fingertips, and God himself is as close as our whispered prayers.

(II Thessalonians 2:16, 17 KJV)

33. How does God give us comfort?

“Yea, though I walk through the valley of the shadow of death, I will fear no evil: for thou art with me; thy rod and thy staff they comfort me.”

(Psalm 23:4 KJV)

“Blessed are they that mourn: for they shall be comforted.”

(Matthew 5:4 KJV)

“He healeth the broken in heart, and bindeth up their wounds.”

(Psalm 147:3 KJV)

“And Moses said unto the people, Fear ye not, stand still, and see the salvation of the LORD, which he will shew to you to day: for the Egyptians whom ye have seen to day, ye shall see them again no more for ever.”

(Exodus 14:13 KJV)

"The Lord upholdeth all that fall, and raiseth up all those that be bowed down."

(Psalm 145:14 KJV)

"These things I have spoken unto you, that in me ye might have peace. In the world ye shall have tribulation: but be of good cheer; I have overcome the world."

(John 16:33 KJV)

"Casting all your care upon him; for he careth for you."

(I Peter 5:7 KJV)

"Fear thou not; for I am with thee: be not dismayed; for I am thy God: I will strengthen thee; yea, I will help thee; yea, I will uphold thee with the right hand of my righteousness."

(Isaiah 41:10 KJV)

"In the day when I cried thou answered me, and strengthened me with strength in my soul."

(Psalm 138:3 KJV)

“The LORD will strengthen him upon the bed of languishing: thou wilt make all his bed in his sickness.”

(Psalm 41:3 KJV)

“And we know that all things work together for good to them that love God, to them who are the called according to his purpose.”

(Romans 8:28 KJV)

God comforts when we wonder about our future plans.

34. How can we comfort others?

“”Blessed be God, even the Father of our Lord Jesus Christ, the Father of mercies, and the God of all comfort;”

“Who comforteth us in all our tribulation, that we may be able to comfort them which are in any trouble, by the comfort wherewith we ourselves are comforted of God.”

The comforted turns into the comforter. That is the job God has for us. As he comforts us in a tough situation, so we comfort others.

(II Corinthians 1:3, 4 KJV)

PROMISE FROM GOD

“The LORD is good, a strong hold in the day of trouble; and he knoweth them that trust in him.”

(Nahum 1:7 KJV)

COMPASSION

35. What can we learn about God’s compassion in helping us be more compassionate?

“And be ye kind one to another, tenderhearted, forgiving one another, even as God for Christ’s sake hath forgiven you.”

(Ephesians 4:32 KJV)

“It is of the LORD’s mercies that we are not consumed, because his compassion fail not.”

"They are new every morning; great is thy faithfulness."

(Lamentations 3:22, 23 KJV)

"And Jesus moved with compassion, put forth his hand, and touched him, and saith unto him, I will; be thou clean."

(Mark 1:41 KJV)

"Be ye therefore merciful, as your Father also is merciful."

(Luke 6:36 KJV)

"For he shall deliver the needy when he crieth; the poor also, and him that hath no helper."

"He shall spare the poor and needy, and shall save souls of the needy."

"He shall redeem their soul from deceit and violence: and precious shall their blood be in his sight."

A sign of godliness is to share the compassionate heart of Jesus. If we want to be like him, we need to be compassionate.

(Psalm 72: 12-14 KJV)

36. Will God's compassion come to us though we do not deserve it?

"The LORD is merciful and gracious, slow to anger and plenteous in mercy."

(Psalm 103:8 KJV)

"This I recall to my mind, therefore have I hope."

"It is of the LORD's mercies that we are not consumed, because his compassions fail not."

(Lamentations 3:21,22 KJV)

PROMISE FROM GOD

"For he shall deliver the needy when he crieth; the poor also, and him that hath no helper."

(Psalm 72:12 KJV)

COMPETITION

37. Should Christians avoid competition?

"And Adam knew Eve his wife; and she conceived, and bare Cain, and said, I have gotten a man from the LORD."

"And she again bare his brother Abel. And Abel was a keeper of sheep, but Cain was a tiller of the ground."

"And in process of time it came to pass, that Cain brought of the fruit of the ground an offering unto the LORD."

"And Abel, he also brought of the firstlings of his flock and of the fat thereof. And the LORD had respect unto Abel and to his offering:"

"But unto Cain and to his offering he had not respect, And Cain was very wroth, and his countenance fell."

"And the LORD said unto Cain, Why art thou wroth? And why is they countenance fallen?"

"If thou doest well, shalt thou not be accepted? And if thou doest not well, sin lieth at the door. And unto thee shall be his desire, and thou shalt rule over him."

"And Cain talked with Abel his brother; and it came to pass, when they were in the field, that Cain rose up against Abel his brother, and slew him."

The LORD acknowledged Abel's contribution (offering), accepted, yet he didn't acknowledge Cain's.

This drove Cain exceptionally angry and dejected.... Can assaulted and slaughtered his brother.

(Genesis 4:1-8 KJV)

"AND it came to pass after this, that Ab'-sa-lom prepared him chariots and horses, and fifty men to run before him."

"And Ab'-sa-lom rose up early, and stood beside the way of the gate: and it was so, that when any man that had a controversy came to the king for judgment, then Ab'-sa-lom called unto him, and said, Of what city art thou? And he said, Thy servant is of one of the tribes of Israel."

"And Ab'-sa-lom said unto him, See, thy matters are good and right; but there is no man deputed of the king to hear thee."

"Ab'-sa-lom said moreover, oh that I were judge in the land, the every man which hath any suit or cause might come unto me, and I would do him justice!"

And it was so, that when any man came nigh to him to do him obeisance, he put forth his hand, and took him, and kissed him."

And on this manner did Ab'-sa-lom to all Israel that came to the king for judgment; so Ab'-sa-lom stole the hearts of the men of Israel."

"And it came to pass after forty years, that Ab'-sa-lom said unto the king, I pray thee, let me go and pay my vow, which I have vowed unto the LORD, in He'-bron."

"For thy servant vowed a vow while I abode at Ge'-shur in Syria, saying, If the LORD shall bring me again indeed to Jerusalem, then I will serve the LORD."

"And the king said unto him, Go in peace. So he arose, and went to He'-bron."

"But Ab'-sa-lom sent spies throughout all the tribes of Israel, saying, As soon as ye hear the sound of the trumpet, then ye shall say, Ab'-sa-lom reigneth in Hb'-bron."

"And with Ab'-sa-lom went two hundred men out of Jerusalem, that were called; and they went in their simplicity, and they knew not any thing."

"And Ab'-sa-lom sent for A-hith'-o-phel the Gi'-lo-nite, David's counsellor, from his city, even from Gi'-loh, while he offered sacrifices. And the conspiracy was strong; for the people increased continually with Ab'-sa-lom."

Lost pride and competitiveness can prompt sin and demolish families, as it did for Absalom's situation.

(II Samuel 15:1-12 KJV)

"Know ye not that they which run in a race run all, but one receiveth the prize? So run, that ye may obtain."

"And every man that striveth for the mastery is temperate in all things. Now they do it to obtain a corruptible crown; but we an incorruptible."

"I therefore so run, not as uncertainly; so fight I, not as one that beateth the air:"

"But I keep under my body, and bring it into subjection; lest that by any means, when I have preached to others, I myself should be a castaway."

You likewise should run so that you will win... appropriately engaged competitive drives can create extraordinary outcomes.

(I Corinthians 9:24-27 KJV)

"But by the grace of God I am what I am: and his grace which was bestowed upon me was not in vain; but I laboured more abundantly than they all; yet not I, but the grace of God which was with me."

"Therefore whether it were I or they, so we preach, and so ye believed."

Paul had an unmistakable serious streak (competitive streak), yet he looked for consistently to praise his Lord as opposed to declare his own superiority.

(I Corinthians 15:10, 11 KJV)

38. People sometimes say I am too competitive. How can I learn to lighten up?

"Lay not up for yourselves treasures upon earth, where moth and rust doth corrupt, and where thieves break through and steal:"

But lay up for yourselves treasures in heaven, where neither moth nor rust doth corrupt, and where thieves do not break through nor steal:"

"For where your treasure is, there will your heart be also."

We are cautioned not to spend our lives competing for inappropriate things for an inappropriate reasons (wrong things for wrong reasons).

(Matthew 6:19-21 KJV)

"Servants, obey in all things your masters according to the flesh; not with eye service, as menpleasers; but in singleness of heart, fearing God:"

"And whatsoever ye do, do it heartily, as to the Lord, and not unto men;"

"Knowing that of the Lord ye shall receive the reward of the inheritance: for ye serve the Lord Christ."

But he that doeth wrong shall receive for the wrong which he hath done: and there is no respect of persons."

We are to drive ourselves to put forth a valiant effort (to do our best), not to beat others, but because our best honors the God who made us.

(Colossians 3:22-25 KJV)

PROMISE FROM GOD

"But thanks be to God, which giveth us the victory through our Lord Jesus Christ."

How we say thanks to God who gives us victory over wrongdoing (sin) and death through Jesus Christ our Lord!

(I Corinthians 15:57 KJV)

COMPLACENCY

39. What causes us to become complacent?

"I did know thee in the wilderness, in the land of great drought."

"According to their pasture, so were they filled; they were filled, and their heart was exalted; therefore have they forgotten me."

I took care of you in the wild, in that dry and parched land. Be that as it may, when you had eaten and were satisfied, you got proud and overlooked (forgot) me.

When we were in need, we for the most part pay attention to God more. Be that as it may, when we are well fed, comfortable, and prosperous, it is simpler to get careless (forget) about God. Savvy (wise) is the individual who remembers God day by day in the midst of both need and success.

(Hosea 13:5, 6 KJV)

40. Is being complacent a sin, particularly complacent toward sin?

"Therefore to him that knoweth to do good, and doeth it not, to him it is sin."

God pay attention to rightness. So should God's people. To realize what is correct and afterward be complacent about it or reluctant to do it is sin.

(James 4:17 KJV)

"And it came to pass, when she pressed him daily with her words, and urged him, so that his soul was vexed unto death;"

'That he told her all his heart, and said unto her, There hath not come a razor upon mine head; for I have been a Nazarite unto God from my mother's womb: if I be shaven, then my strength will go from me, and I shall become weak, and be like any other man."

Samson had become so complacent about his undeniable duty as a leader that he yielded (uncovered the mystery of his strength) and told Deliah. He figured it wouldn't make any difference; he figured everything would in any case be fine. Samson's complaceny was a transgression (sin), since he disobeyed God's command not to leave his hair alone shaved, and he let down his whole country.

(Judges 16:16, 17 KJV)

"But king Solomon loved many strange women, together with the daughter of Pharaoh, women of the Mo'-ab-ites, Am'-mon-ites, E'-dom-ites, Zi-do'-ni-ans, and Hit'-tites;"

"Of the nations concerning which the LORD said unto the children of Israel, Ye shall not go in to them, neither shall they come in unto you: for surely they will turn away your heart after their gods: Solomon clave unto these in love."

"And he had seven hundred wives, princesses, and three hundred concubines: and his wives turned away his heart."

"For it came to pass, when Solomon was old, that his wives turned away his heart after other gods: and his heart was not perfect with the LORD his God, as was the heart of David his father."

King Solomon loved numerous outside women...The LORD had unmistakably taught his people not to intermarry with those nations. However, Solomon insisted on loving them in any case. Also, for sure, they drove his heart away from the LORD.

Solomon's lack of concern (complacency) toward God and God's commands drove him into transgression (sin) and its overwhelming consequences.

(I Kings 11:1-4 KJV)

PROMISE FROM GOD

"I Know thy works, that thou art neither cold nor hot: I would thou wert cold or hot."

"So then because thou art lukewarm, and neither cold nor hot, I will spue thee out of my mouth."

"Because thou sayest, I am rich, and increased with goods, and have need of nothing; and knowest not that thou art wretched, and miserable, and poor, and blind, and naked:"

I know all the things you do, that you are neither hot nor cold. I wish you were either! In any case, since you are like lukewarm water, I will spit you out of my mouth!

(Revelation 3:15-17 KJV)

COMPLAINING

41. Why do people complain?

"And the mixt multitude that was among them fell a lusting: and the children of Israel also wept again, and said, Who shall give us flesh to eat?"

"We remember the fish, which we did eat in Egypt freely; the cucumbers, and the melons, and the leeks, and the onions, and the garlick:"

"But now our soul is dried away; there is nothing at all, beside this man'-na, before our eyes."

The people of Israel began to complain. For some meat! They complained day after day we have nothing to eat but this manna!

(Numbers 11:4-6 KJV)

"The foolishness of man perverteth his way: and his heart fretteth against the LORD."

People ruin their lives by their own stupidity (foolishness) and afterward they are angry with the Lord.

We gripe (complain) when things don't go our way and we don't get what we need.

(Proverbs 19:3 KJV)

42. Is it a sin to complain?

"And the people spake against God, and against Moses, Wherefore have ye brought us up out of Egypt to die in the wildernesss? for there is no bread, neither is there any water, and our soul loatheth this light bread."

"And the LORD sent fiery serpents among the people, and they bit the people; and much people of Israel died."

(Numbers 21:5, 6 KJV)

"Do all things without murmuring and disputings:"

"That ye may be blameless and harmless, the sons of God, without rebuke, in the midst of a crooked and perverse nation, among whom ye shine as lights in the world;"

Be cautious about crying, grumbling, or griping. At the point when we have such a great amount to be appreciative for thus little to gripe about, yet we decide to whine, God thinks of it as a sin. We are showing a disposition of selfishness (ungratefulness). It was enough of a sin for the Israelites that God punished them with harmful poisonous snakes.

(Philippians 2:14, 15 KJV)

PROMISE FROM GOD

"Let no corrupt communication proceed out of your mouth, but that which is good to the use of edifying, that it may minister grace unto the hearers."

Try not to use foul or oppressive language. Let all that you say be acceptable and supportive, with the goal that your words will be a consolation to the individuals who hear them.

(Ephesians 4:29 KJV)

COMPROMISE

43. How do we live in today's culture without compromising our convictions?

"But Daniel purposed in his heart that he would not defile himself with the portion of the king's meat, nor with the wine which he drank" therefore he requested of the prince of the eunuchs that he might not defile himself."

"Now God had brought Daniel into favour and tender love with the prince of the eunuchs."

"And the prince of the eunuchs said unto Daniel, I fear my lord the king, who hath appointed your meat and your drink: for why should he see your faces worse liking than the children which are of your sort? Then shall ye make me endanger my head to the king."

"Then said Daniel to Mei'-zar, whom the prince of the eunuchs had set over Daniel, Han-a-ni'-ah, Mish'-a-el, and Az-a-ri'ah,"

"Prove thy servants, I beseech thee, ten days; and let them give us pulse to eat, and water to drink."

"Then let our countenance be looked upon before thee, and the countenance of the children that eat of the portion of the king's meat: and as thou seest, deal with thy servants."

"So he consented to them in this matter, and proved them ten days."

"And at the end of ten days their countenances appeared fairer and fatter in flesh than all the children which did eat the portion of the king's meat."

"Thus Mel'-zar took away the portion of their meat, and the wine that they should drink; and gave them pulse."

We should stand up for what is correct and true, however in an aware way. Some of the time, as for Daniel's situation, we are respected for our convictions; and for other times we are most certainly are not.

(Daniel 1:8-16 KJV)

""Take heed to thyself, lest thou make a covenant with the inhabitants of the land whither thou goest, lest it be for a snare in the midst of thee:"

Be extremely cautious never to make settlements, treaties (or concurrences with) individuals in the land where you are going. If you do, you will before long be following their evil ways.

(Exodus 34:12 KJV)

"Whosoever transgresseth, and abideth not in the doctrine of Christ, hath not God. He that abideth in the doctrine of Christ, he hath both the Father and the Son."

"If there come any unto you, and bring not this doctrine, receive him not into your house, neither bid him God speed:"

"For he that biddeth him God speed is partaker of his evil deeds."

If you meander past the teaching of Christ, you won't have fellowship with God...

A little sin is similarly as terrible as a great deal of Sin. Sin will be sin, and sin is not right (but rebellion and disobedience against God).

(II John 1:9-11 KJV)

44. Are there relationships, partnerships, and alliances that can quickly lead us to compromise?

"Be nor unequally yoked together with unbelievers: for what fellowship hath righteousness with unrighteousness? And what communion hath light with darkness?"

"And what concord hath Christ with Be'-li-al? Or what part hath he that believeth with an infidel?"

Try not to collaborate with the individuals who are unbelievers. In what capacity would goodness be able to be a collaborate with insidiousness (evil or wickedness)? By what means can light live with darkness? What harmony can there be among Christ and the Devil? How can a believer be a band together (partner) with an unbeliever?

(II Corinthians 6:14, 15 KJV)

"Now Je-hosh'-a-phat had riches and honour in abundance, and joined affinity with Ahab."

(II Chronicles 18:1 KJV)

"Now when the adversaries of Judah and Benjamin heard that the children of the captivity builded the temple unto the LORD God of Israel;"

Then they came to Ze-rub'-ba-bel, and to the chief of the fathers, and said unto them, Let us build with you: for we seek your God, as ye do; and we do sacrifice unto him since the days of E'-sar-had'-don king of As'-sur, which brought us up hither."

(Ezra 4:1, 2 KJV)

"And be not conformed to this world: but be transformed by the renewing of your mind, that ye may prove what is that good, and acceptable, and perfect, will of God."

Do not to duplicate the conduct and customs of this world, however let God change you into a new person.

Partnership, in business or marriage, is collaborating with another to go about as one. God cautions against a partnership in which one loves God and the other doesn't, for in what capacity can these two distinctive conviction frameworks (different belief systems) go about as one?

(Romans 12:2 KJV)

PROMISE FROM GOD

"Whosoever therefore shall confess me before men, him will I confess also before my Father which is in heaven."

"But whosoever shall deny me before men, him will I also deny before my Father which is in heaven."

If anyone recognizes (confess) me publicly here on earth, I will openly recognize (confess) that person before my Father in heaven. In any case, If anyone denies me here on earth, I will deny that person before my Father in heaven.

(Matthew 10:32, 33 KJV)

CONFIDENCE

45. Where can I receive my confidence?

"It is better to trust in the LORD than to put confidence in man."

Trust is identified with the level of dependability (trustworthiness). Faith originates from knowing that God is totally dependable (trustworthy).

(Psalm 118:8 KJV)

"The LORD is my light and my salvation; whom shall I fear? The LORD is the strength of my life; of whom shall I be afraid?"

Confidence (Faith) originates from knowing with conviction that we have salvation and that an eternal home awaits us.

(Psalm 27:1 KJV)

"Behold, what manner of love the Father hath bestowed upon us, that we should be called the sons of God: therefore the world knoweth us not, because it knew him not."

Perceive how much our heavenly Father loves us, for he allows us to be called his children. Confidence (Faith) originates from knowing that God loves us unconditionally.

(I John 3:1 KJV)

46. What if I have lost confidence in others, especially those who have broken a trust?

"Confidence in an unfaithful man in time of trouble is like a broken tooth, and a foot out of joint."

Placing trust (confidence) in an untrustworthy person resembles biting with a toothache or strolling on a broken foot.

It is imperative to love others and assume the best about them. Be that as it may, it is silly to rely upon somebody who has a record of failed trust.

(Proverbs 25:19 KJV)

47. When I lose confidence (Faith) in God what happens?

"Oh that I knew where I might find him! that I might come even to his seat!"

At the point when catastrophe strikes, our first tendency is to consider what befallen God (what happened to God, where is he). Pestering questions cause us to scrutinize his love and care for us. Be that as it may, God's love and care are unending. Losing certainty (confidence, faith) in that reality takes care of us at risk for falling from him.

(Job 23:3 KJV)

"Come unto me, all ye that labour and are heavy laden, and I will give you rest."

When you start to question (doubt) God, race to him not away from him. By what other means will you find the amount he truly loves you?

(Matthew 11:28 KJV)

"Let not your heart be troubled; ye believe in God, believe also in me."

"In my Father's house are many mansions; if it were not so, I would have told you. I go to prepare a place for you."

"And if I go and prepare a place for you, I will come again, and receive you unto myself; that where I am, there ye may be also."

Losing certainty (faith) in God may make us relinquish the eternal blessings he is preparing for us.

(John 14:1-3 KJV)

"Now faith is the substance of things hoped for, the evidence of things not seen."

What is faith? Faith is the certain affirmation that what we trust in (hope) will occur. It is the proof of things we can't yet see..

Faith is certain confident assurance that what you believe is truly going to occur. You can be sure beyond a shadow of a doubt God's promises will work out as expected.

(Hebrews 11:1 KJV)

48. What difference is there between good confidence and bad confidence?

"For I know that my redeemer liveth, and that he shall stand at the latter day upon the earth:"

(Job 19:25 KJV)

"Beloved, now are we the sons of God, and it doth not yet appear what we shall be: but we know that, when he shall appear, we shall be like him; for we shall see him as he is."

Great certainty (good confidence) is an acknowledgment and an affirmation that God loves you, that he has given you abilities and blessings and the capacity to use them for him, that he has offered you salvation and eternal life in heaven. Knowing this gives you complete sureness that your life can have meaning now and forever.

(I John 3:2 KJV)

"But when he was strong, his heart was lifted up to his destruction: for he transgressed against the LORD his God, and went into the temple of the LORD to burn incense upon the altar of incense."

At the point when he had become powerful, he likewise became proud, which prompted his downfall.

Pride is the fixing that makes our certainty become cocky and arrogant. In the event that we want to do it without anyone else's help, when we quit looking for God's help - these are the procuring signs that confidence has turned to arrogance.

(II Chronicles 26:16 KJV)

PROMISE FROM GOD

"Blessed is the man that trusteth in the LORD, and whose hope the LORD is."

Be that as it may, blessed are the individuals who trust in the LORD and have made the LORD their expectation (hope) and certainty (confidence).

(Jeremiah 17:7 KJV)

CONFESSION

49. To whom do we confess our sins, God or others?

"Now therefore make confession unto the LORD God of your fathers, and do his pleasure: and separate yourselves from the people of the land, and from the strange wives."

Confess your sin to the LORD, the God of your fathers, and do what he demands.

(Ezra 10:11 KJV)

"And David said unto God, I have sinned greatly, because I have done this thing: but now, I beseech thee, do away the iniquity of thy servant; for I have done very foolishly."

We confess sin to God first, for only God can forgive sin.

(I Chronicles 21:8 KJV)

"Confess your faults one to another, and pray one for another, that ye may be healed. The effectual fervent prayer of a righteous man availeth much."

It very well may be healing to confess sin to each other, particularly if the others are focused on petitioning God for you, empowering you, and supporting you as you look for rebuilding spiritually. It is likewise essential to confess sin to those whom you have wronged.

(James 5:16 KJV)

50. Does God truly forgive sin when we confess it to him?

"I acknowledge my sin unto thee, and mine iniquity have I not hid. I said, I will confess my transgressions unto the LORD; and thou forgavest the iniquity of my sin. Selah."

I confessed my sin to the Lord, and quit attempting to shroud (hid) them. I said to myself, "I will confess my disobedience (sin) to the LORD." And you forgave me! All my blame is no more.

(Psalm 32:5 KJV)

"If we confess our sins, he is faithful and just to forgive us our sins, and to cleanse us from all unrighteousness."

With sin comes a sentiment of guilt. It's a part of the baggage that sin brings. Confession is the act of perceiving those sins before God so he can forgive them.

(I John 1:9 KJV)

51. Ultimately everyone will confess Jesus as Lord and Saviour, but someday will it be too late to receive his forgiveness?

"That at the name of Jesus every knee should bow, of things in heaven, and things in earth, and things under the earth;"

"And that every tongue should confess that Jesus Christ is Lord, to the glory of God the Father."

(Philippians 2:10, 11 KJV)

"And whosoever was not found written in the book of life was cast into the lake of fire."

Someday every person will bow and confess that Jesus Christ is Lord. In any case, what bitterness, what sadness to make this confession just when we have at long last perceived the inevitable actuality (the inescapable fact) that Jesus truly is Lord - and we have never accepted him all things considered.

(Revelation 20:15 KJV)

PROMISE FROM GOD

"That if thou shalt confess with thy mouth the Lord Jesus, and shalt believe in thine heart that God hath raised him from the dead, thou shall be saved."

(Romans 10:9 KJV)

CONFLICT

52. How does conflict begin?

"And it came to pass after this, that Ab'-sa-lom prepared him chariots and horses, and fifty men to run before him."

"And Ab'-sa-lom rose up early, and stood beside the way of the gate: and it was so, that when any man that when any man that had a controversy came to the king for judgment, then Ab'-sa-lom called unto him, and said, Thy servant is of one of the tribes of Israel."

"And Ab'-sa-lom said unto him, See, thy matters are good and right; but there is no man deputed of the king to hear thee."

"Ab'-sa-lom said moreover, Oh that I made judge in the land, that every man which hath any suit or cause might come unto me, and I would do him justice!"

"And it was so, tht when any man came nigh to him to do him obeisance, he put forth his hand, and took him, and kissed him."

"And on this manner did Ab'-sa-lom to all Israel that came to the king for judgment; so Ab'-sa-lom stole the hearts of the men of Israel."

"And it came to pass after forty years, that Ab'-sa-lom said unto the king, I pray thee, let me go and pay my vow, which I have vowed unto the LORD, in He'-bron."

"For thy servant vowed a vow while I abode at Ge'-shur in Syria, saying, If the LORD shall bring me again indeed to Jerusalem, then I will serve the LORD."

"And the king said unto him, Go in peace. So he arose, and went to He'-bron."

"But Ab-'sa-lom sent spies throughout all the tribes of Israel, saying, As soon as ye hear the sound of the trumpet, then ye shall say, Ab'-sa-lom reigneth in He'-bron."

"And with Ab'-sa-lom went two hundred men out of Jerusalem, that were called; and they went in their simplicity, and they knew not any thing."

"And Ab'-sa-lom sent for A-hith'-o-phel the Gi'-lo-nite, David's counsellor, from his city, even from Gi'-loh, while he offered sacrifices. And the conspiracy was strong; for the people increased continually with Ab'-sa-lom."

Ab'-sa'lom stole the hearts of the people and the conspiracy increased (gained momentum).

Conflict starts when we don't get what we want, and the best way to get it is to take it from another person. This prompts indifference and can prompt open fighting.

(II Samuel 15:1-12 KJV)

"And some days after Paul said unto Barnabas, Let us go again and visit our brethren in every city where we have preached the word of the Lord, and see how they do."

"And Barnabas determined to take with them John, whose surname was Mark."

"But Paul thought not good to take him with them, who departed from them from Pam-phyl'-i-a, and went not with them to the work."

"And the contention was so sharp between them, that they departed asunder one from the other: and so Barnabas took Mark, and sailed unto Cyprus;"

"And Paul chose Silas, and departed, being recommended by the brethren unto the grace of God."

"And he went through Syria and Ci-li'-ci-a, confirming the churches."

They separated because of their disagreement over this.

Conflict starts when two contradicting perspectives are not ready to discover shared opinion (common ground).

(Acts 15:36-41 KJV)

"After these things did king A-has-u-e'-rus promote Ha'-man the son of Ham-med'-a-tha the A'-gag-ite, and advanced him, and set his seat above all the princes that were with him."

And all the king's servants, that were in the king's gate, bowed, and reverend Ha'-man: for the king had so commanded concerning him. But Mor'-de-cai bowed not, nor did him reverence."

Then the king's servants, which were in the king's gate, said unto Mor'-de-cai, Why transgressest thou the king's commandment?"

"Now it came to pass, when they spake daily unto him, and he hearkened not unto them, that they told Ha'-man, to see whether Mor'-de-cai's matters would stand; for he had told them that he was a Jew."

"And when Ha'-man saw that Mor'-de-cai bowed not, nor did him reverence, then was Ha'-man full of wrath."

"And he thought scorn to lay hands on Mor'-de-cai alone; for they had shewed him the people of Mor'-de-cai: wherefore Ha'-man sought to destroy all the Jews that were throughout the whole kingedom of A-has-u-e'-rus, even the people of Mor'-de-cai."

"In the first month, that is, the month Ni'-san, in the twelfth year of king A-has-u-e'rus. They cast Pur, that is, the lot, before Ha'-man from day to day, and from month to month, to the twelfth month, that is, the month A'-dar."

"Anhd ha'-man said unto the king A-has-u-e'rus, There is a certain people scattered abroad and dispersed among the people in all the provinces of thy kingdom; and their laws are diverse from all people; neither keep they the king's laws; therefore it is not for the king's profit to suffer them."

"If it please the king, let it be written that they may be destroyed: and I will pay ten thousand talents of silver to the hands of those that have the charge of the business to bring it into the king's treasuries."

Mordecai would not bow... (Herman) was filled anger. So he concluded it was insufficient (not enough) to lay hands on Mordecai alone...He chose to demolish all the Jews all through the whole empire.

Conflict starts when we look for vengeance (revenge).

(Esther 3:1-9 KJV)

"For we know that the law is spiritual; but I am carnal, sold under sin."

"For that which I do I allow not: for what I would, that do I not; but what I hate, that do I."

"If then I do that which I would not, I consent unto the law that it is good."

"Now then it is no more I that do it, but sin that dwelleth in me."

"For I know that in me (that is, in my flesh,) dwelleth no good thing; for to will is present with me; but how to perform that which is good I find not."

"For the good that I would do not: but the evil which I would not, that I do."

"Now if I do that I would not, it is no more I that do it, but sin that dwelleth in me."

"I find then a law, that, when I would do good, evil is present with me."

"For I delight in the law of God after the inward man:"

"But I see another law in my members, warring against the law of my mind, and bringing me into captivity to the law of sin which is in my members."

"O wretched man that I am! Who shall deliver me from the body of this death?"

"I thank God through Jesus Christ our Lord. So then with the mind I myself serve the law of God; but with the flesh the law of sin."

At the point when I need to do good, I don't. Furthermore, when I do whatever it takes not to foul up (do wrong, sin), I do it in anyway.

Conflict starts when good goes up against evil. The two can't peacefully exist together. One must triumph.

(Romans 7:14-25 KJV)

53. What are a few ways to resolve conflict?

"And there was a strife between the herdmen of Abram's cattle and the herdmen of Lot's cattle: and the Ca'-naan-ite and the Per'-iz-zite dwelled then in the land."

"And Abram said unto Lot, Let there be no strife, I pray thee, between me and thee, and between my herdsmen and thy herdsmen; for we be brethren."

"Is not the whole land before thee? Separate thyself, I pray thee, from me: if thou wilt take the left hand, then I will go to the right; or if thou depart to the right hand, then I will go to the left."

Abram said, this arguing has got to stop between our herdsmen. I'll tell you what we'll do…

In solving conflict someone must step up to the plate and somebody must make the main move. Abram gave Lot first choice, placing family peace above personal desires.

(Genesis 13:7-9 KJV)

"And Isaac departed thence, and pitched his tent in the valley of Ge'-rar, and dwelt there."

"And Isaac digged again the wells of water, which they had digged in the days of Abraham his father; for the Phi-lis'-tines had stopped them after the death of Abraham; and he called their names after the names by which his father had called them."

"And Isaac's servants digged in the valley, and found there a well of springing water."

"And the herdsmen of Ge'-rar did strive with Isaac's herdmen, saying, The water is our's: and he called the name of the well E'-sek; because they strove with him."

And they digged another well, and strove for that also; and he called the name of it Sit'-nah."

"And he removed from thence, and digged another well; and for that they strove not: and he called the name of it Re-ho'-both; and he said, For now the LORD hath made room for us, and we shall be fruitful in the land."

Isaac's men at that point burrowed another well, yet again there was a battle about it...he burrowed another well, and the nearby individuals at long last let him alone.

Solving conflict take quietude, a longing to see harmony (peace) more than personal triumph.

(Genesis 26:17-22 KJV)

"Now there was long war between the house of Saul and the house of David: but David waxed stronger and stronger, and the house of Saul waxed weaker and weaker."

This was the beginning of a long war between those who had been loyal to Saul and those who had been loyal to David.

Tackling (solving) conflict includes compromise, discovering shared belief (common ground) that is greater than your disparities.

In the event that neither one of the sides is eager to step up to the plate or demonstrate the important lowliness to look for shared conviction, struggle will bring about a messed up friendship, divorce, or even war.

(II Samuel 3:1 KJV)

54. How must I keep a conflict from getting out of hand (out of control)?

"He hath knowledge spareth his words: and a man of understanding is of an excellent spirit."

Words can be used as tools or weapons and subsequently should be utilized cautiously.

(Proverbs 17:27 KJV)

"Therefore if thou bring thy gift to the altar, and there rememberest that thy brother hath ought against thee;"

"Leave there thy gift before the altar, and go thy way; first be reconciled to thy brother, and then come and offer thy gift."

"Agree with thine adversary quickly, whiles thou art in the way with him; lest at any time the adversary deliver thee to the judge, and the judge deliver the to the officer, and thou be cast into prison."

"Verily I say unto thee, Thou shalt by no means come out thence, till thou hast paid the uttermost farthing."

We are not to bury" or deny conflicts (clashes), but instead to find a way in taking steps to resolve them.

(Matthew 5:23-26 KJV)

"Moreover if thy brother shall trespass against thee, go and tell him his fault between the and him alone: if he shall hear thee, thou hast gained thy brother."

"But if he will not hear thee, then take with thee one or two more, that in THE MOUTH OF TWO OR THREE WITNESSES EVERY WORD MAY BE ESTABLISHED."

"And if he shall neglect to hear them, tell it unto the church, let him be unto thee as an heathen man and a publican."

Jesus outlines a three-step process for confronting major conflicts among believers.

(Matthew 18:15-17 KJV)

"Now I beseech you, brethren, mark them which cause divisions and offences contrary to the doctrine which ye have learned; and avoid them."

Often time the best way to deal with conflict is to "AVOID" it.

(Romans 16:17 KJV)

PROMISE FROM GOD

"Ye have heard that it hath been said, THOU SHALT LOVE THY NEIGHBOR, and hate thine enemy."

"But I say unto you, Love your enemies, bless them that curse you, do good to them that hate you, and pray for them which despitefully use you, and persecute you;"

"That ye may be the children of your Father which is in heaven; for he maketh his sun to rise on the evil and on the good, and sendeth rain on the just and on the unjust."

You have heard that the law of Moses says, "Love your neighbor and hate your enemy." But I state, Love your enemy! Pray to God for the individuals who mistreat you! In that manner, you will be going about as the true offspring of your Father in paradise...

(Matthew 5:43-45 KJV)

CONSEQUENCES

55. God gives us the freedom to choose what we want to do, but what are the consequences of choosing to sin?

"For wages of sin is death; but the gift of God is eternal life through Jesus Christ our Lord."

The greatest result of transgression (sin) is endless (eternal) detachment (separation) from God.

(Romans 6:23 KJV)

"And when the woman saw that the tree was good for food, and that it was pleasant to the eyes, and a tree to be desired to make one wise, she took of the fruit thereof, and did eat, and gave also unto her husband with her; and he did eat."

"And the eyes of both were opened, and they knew that they were naked; and they sewed fig leaves together, and made themselves aprons."

"Unto the woman he said, I will greatly multiply thy sorrow and thy conception; in sorrow thou shalt bring forth children; and thy desire shall be to thy husband, and he shall rule over thee."

"And unto Adam he said, Because thous hast hearkened unto the voice of thy wife, and hast eaten of the tree, of which I commanded thee, saying, Thou shalt not eat of it; cursed is the ground for thy sake; in sorrow shalt thou eat of it all the days of thy life;"

"Thorns also and thistles shall it bring forth to thee; and thou shalt eat the herb of the field;"

"In the sweat of thy face shalt thou eat bread, till thou return unto the ground; for out of it wast thou taken: for dust thou art, and unto dust shalt thou return."

Indeed, even an apparently little sin must be taken a look at for what it is: defiance or disobedience to God. One of the real factors of transgression (sin) is that its impact spreads, and soon the pattern of results is turning a long ways outside our ability to control.

(Genesis 3:6, 7; 16-19 KJV)

"How much better is it to get wisdom than gold! And to get understanding rather to be chosen than silver!"

It is safe to say that you will take care of a specific activity? God doesn't keep us from acting absurdly; he just helps us to remember the results of silliness, foolishness.

(Proverbs 16:16 KJV)

"Be not deceived; God is not mocked: for whatsoever a man soweth, that shall he reap."

Sin isn't right (it's wrong), so it generally produces terrible or awful consequences.

(Galatians 6:7 KJV)

56. Is it true that we share the consequences for another person's failure or sin?

"And Joshua said, Why hast thou troubled us? The LORD shall trouble thee this day. And all Israel stoned him with stones, and burned them with fire, after they had stoned them with stones."

Our corrupt (sinful) activities influence a larger number of people than just ourselves. Be careful with the impulse to defend your transgressions (sins) by saying they are excessively little or too personal to even consider hurting anybody but you.

(Joshua 7:25 KJV)

"Again, When a righteous man doth turn from his righteousness, and commit iniquity, and I lay a stumblingblock before him, he shall die; because thou hast not given him warning, he shall die in his sin, and his righteousness which he hath done shall not be remembered; but his blood will I require at thine hand."

In the event that good individuals turn awful and don't tune in to my warning, they will die. If that you didn't caution them of the consequences, at that point they will die in their sins...and I will hold you responsible..."

A guard (watchman) is liable in the event that he realizes the adversary is coming and stays quiet. We are liable if we stay quiet (silent) when we ought to caution someone else of the consequences of his or her actions.

(Ezekiel 3:20 KJV)

PROMISE FROM GOD

"Whoso rewardeth evil for good, evil shall not depart from his house."

(Proverbs 17:13 KJV)

57. Can the consequences of what we say be just as significant as the consequences of what we do?

"Death and life are in the power of the tongue: and they that love it shall eat the fruit thereof."

Those individuals who love to talk will experience the consequences, for the tongue can slaughter (kill) or support (nourish) life.

(Proverbs 18:21 KJV)

"And as Peter was beneath in the palace, there cometh one of his maids of the high priest:"

"And when she saw Peter warming himself, she looked upon him, and said, And thou also wast with Jesus of Nazareth."

"But he denied, saying, I know not, neither understand I what thou sayest. And he went out into the porch; and the crock crew."

"And a maid saw him again, and began to say to them that stood by, This is one of them."

"And he denied it again. And a little after, they that stood by said again to Peter, Surely thou art one of them: for thou art a Gal-i-lae'-an, and thy speech agreeth thereto."

"But he began to curse and to swear, saying, I know not this man of whom ye speak."

"And the second time the cock crew. And Peter called to mind the word that Jesus said to him, Before the cock crow twice, thou shalt deny me thrice. And when he thought thereon, he wept."

Loose lips sink ships, and may sink the ships as without a doubt as a enemy torpedo. Spies who pass on imperative data are as blameworthy of the death of guiltless, innocent people as the individuals who pull the triggers. Our words condemn us as vigorously as our actions.

(Mark 14:66-72 KJV)

PROMISE FROM GOD

"Whoso rewardeth evil for good, evil shall not depart from his house."

If you repay evil for good, evil will never leave your house.

(Proverbs 17:13 KJV)

CONTENTMENT

58. How do I find true peace and contentment in life?

"Thou wilt keep him in perfect peace, whose mind is stayed on thee; because he trusteth in thee."

There are numerous approaches to have transient harmony (peace) or what we believe is peace, yet true peace is found uniquely in a confiding in relationship with the Lord.

(Isaiah 26:3 KJV)

"And Esau said, I have enough, my brother; keep that thou hast unto thyself."

A Key way to contentment is to forgive those who have wronged us.

(Genesis 33:9 KJV)

59. Can contentment be found in money or success?

"Every man also to whom God hath given riches and wealth, and hath given him power to eat thereof, and to take his portion, and to rejoice in his labour; this is the gift of God."

"For he shall not much remember the days of his life; because God answereth him in the joy of his heart."

To appreciate (enjoy) work and acknowledge your current situation - that is to be sure a blessing from God. People who do this once in a while (rarely) look with distress (sorrow) on the past, for God has given them explanations for joy.

(Ecclesiastes 5:19, 20 KJV)

"Not that I speak in respect of want: for I have learned, in whatsoever state I am, therewith to be content."

"I know both how to be abased, and I know how to abound: every where and in all things I am instructed both to be full and to be hungry, both to abound and to suffer need." "I can do all things through Christ which strengtheneth me."

(Philippians 4:11-13 KJV)

"Let your conversation be without covetousness; and be content with such things as ye have: for he hath said, I WILL NEVER LEAVE THEE, NOR FORSAKE THEE."

Avoid the love for money; be happy with what you have. For God has stated, "I will never fail you. I will never neglect you."

Contentment isn't subject to riches (wealth), nor does it need to be smothered by destitution (poverty). Wealth without anyone else's input is unbiased - neither good nor bad. The key is to express gratitude (thanks) to God for what we have and to utilize our time and assets to please him.

(Hebrews 13:5 KJV)

"Be sobeer, be vigilant; because your adversary the devil, as a roaring lion, walketh about, seeking whom he may devour:"

Satan will likely get us to accept (or to believe) the illusion that knowing more or having more will make us content (this is Satan's goal). As a matter of fact, it just shows we'll never be satisfied. An individual who is forever discontent is an individual who neglects to completely confide (trust in) in God.

(I Peter 5:8 KJV)

“But godliness with contentment is great gain.”

“For we brought nothing into this world, and it is certain we can carry nothing out.”

Knowing that our real home is with God in time everlasting (heaven) should assist us with being content with what we have now. Making wise personal investments here will bring us great wealth in heaven.

(I Timothy 6:6, 7 KJV)

60. How do I learn to be content in any situation?

“Blessed are the poor in spirit: for their’s is the kingdom of heaven.”

God blesses the individuals who understand their need for him, for the Kingdom of Heaven is given to them.

(Matthew 5:3 KJV)

"So likewise, whosoever he be of you that forsaketh not all that he hath, he cannot be my disciple."

No one can become my disciple without giving up everything for me.

Contentment comes when we are eager to give up everything for God. Only then are we really allowed to rest in the harmony (peace) and security God offers.

(Luke 14:33 KJV)

PROMISE FROM GOD

"For he satisfieth the longing soul, and filleth the hungry soul with goodness."

For he satisfies the thirsty and fills the hungry with good things.

(Psalm 107:9 KJV)

CONTROL

61. With everything out of control in the world, how can people still say "God is in control"?

"Then Paul stood in the midst of Mars' hill, and said, Ye men of Athens, I perceive that in all things ye are too superstitious."

"For as I passed by, and beheld your devotions, I found an altar with this inscription, TO THE UNKNOWN GOD. Whom therefore ye ignorantly worship, him declare I unto you."

God that made the world and all things therein, seeing that he is Lord of heaven and earth, dwelleth not in temples made with hands;"

"Neither is worshipped with men's hands, as though he needed any thing, seeing he giveth to all life, and breath, and all things;"

"And hath made of one blood all nations of men for to dwell on all the face of the earth, and hath determined the times before appointed, and the bounds of their habitation;"

"That they should seek the Lord, if haply they might feel after him, and find him, though he be not far from every one of us:"

"For in him we live, and move, and have our being; as certain also of your own poets have said, For we are also his offspring."

"Forasmuch then as we are the offspring of God, we ought not to think that the Godhead is like unto gold, silver, or stone, graven by art and man's device."

"And the times of this ignorance God winked at; but now commandeth all men every where to repent:"

"Because he hath appointed a day, in the which he will judge the world in righteousness by that man whom he hath ordained; whereof he hath given assurance unto all men, in that he hath raised him from the dead."

He has set a day for judging the world with justice.

Despite the fact that we may not comprehend the transgression (sin) and abhorrence (evil) in this world, we can believe the Lord of heaven and earth to one day work out his great redemptive purpose.

(Acts 17:22-31 KJV)

"Who is the image of the invisible God, the firstborn of every creature:"

"For by him were all things created, that are in heaven, and that are in earth, visible and invisible, whether they be thrones, or dominions, or principalities, or powers; all things were created by him, and for him:"

"And he is before all things, and by him all things consist."

In other words, He existed before everything else began, and he holds all creation together.

Jesus Christ is Lord even of all concealed spiritual powers and can be trusted with the ultimate control of the universe.

(Colossians 1:15-17 KJV)

"And what is the exceeding greatness of his power to us-ward who believe, according to the working of his mighty power,"

"Which he wrought in Christ, when he raised him from the dead, and set him at his own right hand in the heavenly places,"

“Far above all principality, and power, and might, and dominion, and every name that is named, not only in this world, but also in that which is to come:”

“And hath put all things under his feet, and gave him to be the head over all things to the church,”

“Which is his body, the fulness of him that filleth all in all.”

God has put all things under the authority of Jesus Christ, and he gave him this authority for the benefit of the church.

By the same power that raised him from the dead, Jesus Christ will one day bring everything under His sovereign control.

(Ephesians 1:19-23 KJV)

“And, THOU, LORD, IN THE BEGINNING HAST LAID THE FOUNDATION OF THE EARTH; AND THE HEAVENS ARE THE WORKS OF THINE HANDS:”

“THEY SHALL PERISH; BUT THOU REMAINEST; AND THEY ALL SHALL WAX OLD AS DOTH A GARMENT;”

"AND AS A VESTURE SHALT THOU FOLD THEM UP, AND THEY SHALL BE CHANGED; BUT THOU ART THE SAME, AND THY YEARS SHALL NOT FAIL."

"But to which of the angels said he at any time, SIT ON MY RIGHT HAND, UNTIL I MAKE THINE ENEMIES THY FOOTSTOOL?"

Lord, in the beginning you laid the foundation of the earth, and the heavens are the work of your hands.

Despite the fact that our human viewpoint is restricted, Jesus Christ is the incomparable, supreme ruler of all things.

(Hebrews 1:10-13 KJV)

62. Does the Bible offer me any help in dealing with people who are controlling?

"And Laban said unto Jacob, Because thou art my brother, shouldest thou therefore serve me for nought? tell me, what shall thy wages be?"

"And Laban had two daughters: the name of the elder was Leah, and the name of the younger was Ra'-chel."

"Leah was tender eyed; but Ra'-chel was beautiful and well favoured."

"And Jacob loved Ra'-chel; and said, I will serve thee seven years for Ra'-chel thy younger daughter."

"And Laban said, It is better that I give her to thee, than that I should give her to another man: abide with me."

"And Jacob served seven years for Ra'-chel; and they seemed unto him but a few days, for the love he had to her."

"And Jacob said unto Laban, Give me my wife, for my days are fulfilled, that I may go in unto her."

"And Laban gathered together all the men of the place, and made a feast."

"And it came to pass in the evening, that he took Leah his daughter, and brought her to him; and he went in unto her."

"And Leban gave unto his daughter Leah Zil'-pah his maid for an handmaid."

"And it came to pass, that in the morning, behold, it was Leah: and he said to Leban, What is this thou hast done unto me? did not I serve with thee for Ra'-chel? wherefore then hast thou beguiled me?"

"And Laban said, It must not be so done in our country, to give the younger before the firstborn."

"Fulfil her week, and we will give thee this also for the service which thou shalt serve with me yet seven other years."

"And Jacob did so, and fulfilled her week: and he gave him Ra'-chel his daughter to wife also."

"And Laban gave to Ra'-chel his daughter Bil'-hah his handmaid to be her maid."

"And he went in also unto Ra'-chel, and he loved also Ra'-chel more than Leah, and served with him yet seven other years."

(Genesis 29:15-39 KJV)

"And it came to pass, when Ra'-chel had born Joseph, that Jacob said unto Laban, Send me away, that I may go unto mine own place, and to my country."

"Give me my wives and my children, for whom I have served thee, and let me go: for thou knowest my service which I have done thee."

"And Laban said unto him, I pray thee, if I have found favour in thine eyes, tarry: for I have learned by experience that the LORD hath blessed me for thy sake."

"And he said, Appoint me thy wages, and I will give it."

"And he said unto him, Thou knowest how I have served thee, and how thy cattle was with me."

"For it was little which thou hadst before I came, and it is now increased unto a multitude; and the LORD hast blessed thee since my coming: and now when shall I provide for mine own house also?"

"And he said, What shall I give thee? And Jacob said, Thou shalt not give me any thing: if thou wilt do this thing for me, I will again feed and keep thy flock."

"I will pass through all thy flock to day, removing from thence all the speckled and spotted cattle, and all the brown cattle among the sheep, and the spotted and speckled among the goats: and of such shall be my hire."

"So shall my righteousness answer for me in time to come, when it shall come for my hire before thy face: every one that is not speckled and spotted among the goats, and brown among the sheep, that shall be counted stolen with me."

"And Laban said, Behold, I would it might be according to thy word."

"And he removed that day the he goats that were ringstraked and spotted, and all the she goats that were speckled and spotted, and every one that had some white in it, and all the brown among the sheep, and gave them into the hand of his sons."

"And he set three days' journey betwixt himself and Jacob: and Jacob fed the rest of Laban's flocks."

"And Jacob took him rods of green popar, and of the hazel and chesnut tree; and pilled white strakes in them, and made the white appear which was in the rods."

"And he set the rods which he had pilled before the flocks in the gutters in the watering troughs when the flocks came to drink, that they should conceive when they came to drink."

"And the flocks conceived before the rods, and brought forth cattle ringstraked, speckled, and spotted."

"And Jacob did separate the lambs, and set the faces of the flocks toward the ringstraked, and all the brown in the flock of Laban; and he put his own flocks by themselves, and put them not unto Laban's cattle."

"And it came to pass, whensoever the stronger cattle did conceive, that Jacob laid rods before the eyes of the cattle in the gutters, that they might conceive among the rods."

"But when the cattle were feeble, he put them not in: so the feebler were Laban's, and the stronger Jacob's."

"And the man increased exceedingly, and had much cattle, and maidservants, and menservants, and camels, and asses."

Jacob at last broke liberated from Laban's control by a blend of confrontation, persistence (patience), and shrewd negotiation.

(Genesis 30:25-43 KJV)

"Beloved, thou doest faithfully whatsoever thou doest to the brethren, and to strangers;"

"Which have borne witness of thy charity before the church: whom if thou bring forward on their journey after a godly sort, thou shalt do well:"

"Because that for his name's sake they went forth, taking nothing of the Gentiles."

"We therefore ought to receive such, that we might be fellowhelpers to the truth."

"I wrote unto the church: but Di-ot'-re-phes, who loveth to have the preeminence among them, receiveth us not."

"Wherefore, if I come, I will remember his deeds which he doeth, prating against us with malicious words: and not content therewith, neither doth he himself receive the brethren, and forbiddeth them that would, and casteth them out of the church."

"Beloved, follow not that which is evil, but that which is good. He that doeth good is of God: but he that doeth evil hath not seen God."

Not only does he not welcome the traveling teachers, he also tells other not to help them.

As John advises in this passage, we are to stand up to (confront) the individuals who control others for narrow minded reasons. We should never forfeit truth or the good of the entire church for one narrow minded and controlling individual. Be that as it may, any such confrontation must be dealt with love (see Ephesians 4:15).

(III John 1:5-11 KJV)

"But speaking the truth in love, may grow up into him in all things, which is the head, even Christ:"

(Ephesians 4:15 KJV)

"Howbeit then, when ye knew not God, ye did service unto them which by nature are no gods."

"But now, after that ye have known God, or rather are known of God, how turn ye again to the weak and beggarly elements, whereunto ye desire again to be in bondage?"

"Ye observe days, and months, and times, and years."

(Galatians 4:8-10 KJV)

"They zealously affect you, but not well; yea, they would exclude you, that ye might affect them."

"But it is good to be zealously affected always in a good thing, and not only when I am present with you."

"My little children, of whom I travail in birth again until Christ be formed in you."

"I desire to be present with you now, and to change my voice; for I stand in doubt of you."

Those false teachers who are so anxious to win your favor are not doing it for your good.

Paul went up against (confronted) in the most grounded conceivable language (strongest possible language) those (bogus, false teachers) who looked for inappropriate and ruinous (destructive) control of the early church.

(Galatians 17-20 KJV)

63. How can I learn to have more self-control?

"And beside this, giving all diligence, add to your faith virtue; and to virtue knowledge;"

"And to knowledge temperance; and to temperance patience; and to patience godliness;"

"And to godliness brotherly kindness; and to brotherly kindness charity."

"For if these things be in you, and abound, they make you that ye shall neither be barren nor unfruitful in the knowledge of our Lord Jesus Christ."

Make every effort to apply these to your life... Knowing God leads to self-control. Self-control leads... (Self- control comes only as the product of intentional spiritual growth).

(II Peter 1:5-8 KJV)

"My brethren, be not many masters, knowing that we shall receive the greater condemnation."

"For in many things we offend all. If any man offend not in word, the same is a perfect man, and able also to bridle the whole body."

"Behold, we put bits in the horses mouths, that they may obey us ; and we turn about their whole body."

"Behold also the ships, which though they be great, and are driven of fierce winds, yet are they turned about with a very small helm, whithersoever the governor listeth."

"Even so the tongue is a little member, and boasteth great things. Behold, how great a matter a little fire kindleth!"

"And the tongue is a fire, a world of iniquity; so is the tongue among our members, that it defileth the whole body, and setteth on fire the course of nature; and it is set on fire of hell."

"For every kind of beasts, and of birds, and of serpents, and of things in the sea, is tamed, and hath been tamed of mankind:"

"But the tongue can no man tame; it is an unruly evil, full of deadly poison."

"Therewith bless we God, even the Father; and therewith curse we men, which are made after the similitude of God."

"Out of the same mouth proceedeth blessing and cursing. My brethren, these things ought not so to be."

"Doth a fountain send forth at the same place sweet water and bitter?"

"Can the fig tree, my brethren, bear olive berries? Either a vine, figs? So can no fountain both yield salt water and fresh."

If you can control your tongue you can also control themselves in every other way.

Self-control begins with taming the tongue.

(James 3:1-12 KJV)

"THERE is therefore now no condemnation to them which are in Christ Jesus, who walk not after the flesh, but after the Spirit."

"For the law of the Spirit of life in Christ Jesus hath made me free from the law of sin and death."

"For what the law could not do, in that it was weak through the flesh, God sending his own Son in the likeness of sinful flesh, and for sin, condemned sin in the flesh:"

"That is the righteousness of the law might be fulfilled in us, who walk not after the flesh, but after the Spirit."

"For they that are after the flesh do mind the things of the flesh; but they that are after the Spirit the things of the Spirit."

"For to be carnally minded is death; but to be spiritually minded is life and peace."

"Because the carnal mind is enmity against God: for it is not subject to the law of God; neither indeed can be."

"So they that are in the flesh cannot please God."

"But ye are not in the flesh, but in the Spirit, if so be that the Spirit of God dwell in you. Now if any man have not the Spirit of Christ, he is none of his."

The individuals who are controlled by evil nature consider wicked things, however the individuals who are controlled by the Holy Spirit consider things that please the Spirit.

The best self-control is "Spirit – control."

(Romans 8:1-9 KJV)

"But the fruit of the Spirit is love, joy, peace, longsuffering, gentleness, goodness, faith,"

"Meekness, temperance; against such there is no law."

Self-control is one of the essential characteristics or marks of the Holy Spirit's presence and activity in our lives.

(Galatians 5:22, 23 KJV)

PROMISE FROM GOD

"All nations whom thou hast made shall come and worship before thee, O Lord; and shal glorify thy name."

(Psalm 86:9 KJV)

COOPERATION

64. Are there some guidelines for successful teamwork?

"Thou shalt not plow with an ox and an ass together."

"Thou shalt not wear a garment of divers sorts, as of woollen and linen together."

Choose colleagues who share your essential arrangement of values and assumptionss, else you will pull in different directions.

(Deuteronomy 22:10, 11 KJV)

"Behold, how good and how pleasant it is for brethren to dwell together in unity!"

"It is like the precious ointment upon the head, that ran down upon the beard, even Aaron's beard: that went down to the skirts of his garments;"

How awesome it is, the means by which charming, when brothers live respectively in harmony!...

While helping out others, generally look for solidarity. Differences need not transform into personal attacks.

(Psalm 133:1, 2 KJV)

65. How do I cooperate with someone I don't get along with?

"Iron sharpeneth Iron; so a man sharpeneth the countenance of his friend."

Differences (Differences) can create a positive outcome - to present new thoughts that may challenge and invigorate our thinking.

(Proverbs 27:17 KJV)

"Now I beseech you, brethren, by the name of our Lord Jesus Christ, that ye all speak the same thing, and that there be no divisions among you; but that ye be perfectly joined together in the same mind and in the same judgment."

Loving confrontation is not the same as argumentativeness. Conflict is unavoidable, when it emerges, genuine cooperation looks for the most elevated useful (highest good) for all.

(I Corinthians 1:10 KJV)

66. How do I accomplish cooperation between me and God?

"Commit thy way unto the LORD; trust also in him; and he shall bring it to pass."

Commit everything you do to the LORD. Trust him, and he will help you.

(Psalm 37:5 KJV)

"For God so loved the world, that he gave his only begotten Son, that whosoever believeth in him should not perish, but have everlasting life."

God is offering you right now his unlimited, unconditional love and all the endowments that accompany it. You should simply accept and acknowledge his love, his salvation and, have believe in his Son, Jesus Christ, and live in obedience to his Word (the Bible).

(John 3:16 KJV)

PROMISE FROM GOD

"Two are better than one; because they have a good reward for their labour."

"For if they fall, the one will lift up his fellow; but woe to him that is alone when he falleth; for he hath not another to help him up."

"Again, if two lie together, then they have heat: but how can one be warm alone?"

"And if one prevail against him, two shall withstand him; and a threefold core is not quickly broken."

A Triple-braided cord is not easily broken.

(Ecclesiastes 4:9-12 KJV)

COURAGE

67. When life seems too hard or obstacles seem too big or difficult where do I get the courage to go on?

"When thou goest out to battle against thine enemies, and seest horses, and chariots, and a people more than thou, be not afraid of them: for the LORD thy God is with thee, which brought thee up out of the land of Egypt."

The LORD your God...is with you!

(Deuteronomy 20:1 KJV)

"The LORD is my light and my salvation; whom shall I fear? The LORD is the strength of my life; of whom shall I be afraid?"

Why should I be afraid when the LORD is my light and my salvation?

(Psalm 27:1 KJV)

"Fear thou not; for I am with thee: be not dismayed; for I am thy God: I will strengthen thee; yea, I will help thee; yea, I will uphold thee with the right hand of my righteousness."

Do not be afraid, for I am with you. Do not to be disheartened, for I am your God. I will strengthen you. I will help you. I will maintain you with my victorious right hand.

(Isaiah 41:10 KJV)

"Have not I commanded thee? Be strong and of a good courage; be not afraid, neither be thou dismayed: for the LORD thy God is with thee whithersoever thou goest."

Genuine mental fortitude (true courage) originates from God, understanding that he is stronger than our mightiest enemies and that he wants to use his strength to help us.

(Joshua 1:9 KJV)

68. How do I find courage to face change?

"And he said, I am God, the God of thy father: fear not to go down into Egypt; for I will there make of thee a great nation:"

"I will go down with thee into Egypt; and I will surely bring thee up again: and Joseph shall put his hand upon thine eyes."

Change might be a part of God's arrangement for you. Assuming this is the case, what you are going into will give you joy and fulfillment past your expectations.

(Genesis 46:3, 4 KJV)

"And he said, O my LORD, send, I pray thee, by the hand of him whom thou wilt send."

(Moses wanted and pleaded, "Lord please! Send someone else!")

To experience is typical (normal). To be incapacitated by fear, notwithstanding, can be a sign that you question God's ability to care about you in the face of change.

(Exodus 4:13 KJV)

"And when Saul's son heard that Abner was dead in He'-bron, his hands were feeble, and all the Israelites were troubled."

If you take the entirety of your courage from someone else, you will in the long run be left with nothing when that individual is no more. In the event that you trust in God, you will have the strength to go on in any event, when conditions breakdown (collapse) around you.

(II Samuel 4:1 KJV)

69. How do I find courage to admit my mistakes?

"And David said unto Nathan, I have sinned against the LORD, And Nathan said unto David, The LORD also hath put away thy sin; thou shalt not die."

To admit our mix-ups (mistakes) and sins is to open the entryway to forgiveness and rebuilding of relationships.

(II Samuel 12:13 KJV)

70. Are there consequences to a lack of courage?

"And Pilate, when he had called together the chief priests and the rulers and the people."

"Said unto them, "Ye have brought this man unto me, as one that perverteth the people; and, behold I, having examined him before you, have found no fault in this man touching those things whereof ye accuse him:"

"No, nor yet Herod; for I sent you to him; and, lo, nothing worthy of death is done unto him."

"I will therefore chastise him and release him."

"(For of necessity he must release one unto them at the feast.)"

"And they cried out all at once, saying, Away with this man, and release unto us Bar-ab'-bas:"

"(Who for a certain sedition made in the city, and for murder, was cast into prison.)"

"Pilate therefore, willing to release Jesus, spake again to them."

"But they cried, saying, Crucify him, crucify him."

"Amd he said unto them the third time, Why, what evil hath he done? I have found no cause of death in him: I will therefore chastise him, and let him go."

"And they were instant with loud voices, requiring that he might be crucified. And the voices of them and of the chief priests prevailed."

'And Pilate gave sentence that it should be as they required."

"And he released unto them him that for sedition and murder was cast into prison, whom they had desired but he delivered Jesus to their will."

(The voices of the chief priests and the people prevailed. So Pilate sentenced Jesus to die by crucifixion as they demanded). Supporting (Standing up) what is right can get you in a tough situation from wicked, degenerate individuals (sinful people). Neglecting to defend what is right or to do right can get you in a trouble with God.

(Luke 23:13-25 KJV)

PROMISE FROM GOD

"Have not I commanded thee? Be strong and of a good courage; be not afraid, neither be thou dismayed: for the LORD thy God is with thee whithersoever thou goest."

God commands you to – be strong and courageous! Do not be afraid or discouraged. For the LORD your God is with you wherever you go.

(Joshua 1:9 KJV)

CRITICISM

71. How should I respond to criticism? How may I know whether it is constructive or destructive?

"A fool's wrath is presently known: but a prudent man covereth shame."

"He that speaketh truth sheweth forth righteousness: but a false witness deceit."

"There is that speaketh like the piercings of a sword: but the tongue of the wise is health."

A false witness tells lies, but the words of the wise bring healing.

If you are scrutinized (criticized), remain quiet and don't lash back. Assess whether the analysis is originating from an individual with a reputation for truth or untruths (lies). Ask yourself if the criticism is intended to heal or to hurt.

(Proverbs 12:16-18 KJV)

"It is better to hear the rebuke of the wise, than for a man to hear the song of fools."

It is smarter to be criticized by a savvy (wise) individual than to be commended or praised by a numb-skull (a fool)!

Measure criticism as per the stature of the individual who is giving it.

(Ecclesiastes 7:5 KJV)

"But with me it is a very small thing that I should be judged of you, or of man's judgment: yea, I judge not mine own self."

"For I know nothing by myself; yet am I not hereby justified: but he that judgeth me is the Lord."

"Therefore judge nothing before the time, until the Lord come, who both will bring to light the hidden things of darkness, and will make manifest the counsels of the hearts: and then shall every man have praise of God."

My conscience is clear, however that isn't what makes a difference. It is simply the Lord who will examine me and decide. Continuously work to keep up a clear conscience by being straightforward (honest) and dependable (trustworthy). This permits you to disregard criticism you know is unjustified.

(I Corinthians 4:3-5 KJV)

"If ye are reproached for the name of Christ, happy are ye; for the spirit of glory and of God resteth upon you: on their part he is evil spoken of, but on your part he is glorified."

Be cheerful, or be happy if you are insulted for being a Christian, for then the glorious Spirit of God will come upon you. Think of it as a privilege to be scrutinized, criticized for your faith in God. God has unique blessings for those who quietly persevere (endure) through this sort of criticism.

(I Peter 4:14 KJV)

"The ear that heareth the reproof of life abideth among the wise,"

"He that refuseth instruction despiseth his own soul: but he that heareth reproof getteth understanding."

If you listen to constructive criticism, you will be at home among the wise...

We scam (shortchange) our future when we dismiss honest or truthful data about ourselves. Once in a while it's agonizing (painful) to hear truth, however it's more regrettable (worse) to continue without improvement.

(Proverbs 15:31, 32 KJV)

72. How do we deliver criticism when we feel it must be given?

"So when they continued asking him, he lifted up himself, and said unto them, He that is without sin among you, let him first cast a stone at her."

Let those who have never sinned throw the first stones!

(John 8: KJV 7)

"Therefore thou art inexcusable, O man, whosoever thou art that judgest: for wherein thou judgest another, thou condemnest thyself; for thou that judgest doest the same things."

Before criticizing another person's sins, take inventory of your very own sins and inadequacies so you can move toward the individual with understanding and lowliness (humility).

(Romans 2:1 KJV)

"Doth not behave unseemly, seeketh not her own, is not easily provoked, thinketh no evil:"

Love doesn't demand it's own way. Love isn't bad tempered (irritable), and it keeps no record of when it has been wronged.

Constructive criticism is constantly offered in love, to build up. Furthermore, criticism consistently ought to be responded to in love also.

(I Corinthians 13:5 KJV)

"But why dost thou judge thy brother? Or why dost thou set at nought thy brother? For we shall all stand before the judgment seat of Christ."

So for what reason do you condemn another Christian? Keep in mind, every one of us will stand by and by before the judgment seat of Christ.

(Romans 14:10 KJV)

"JUDGE not, that ye be not judged."

(Stop judging others, and you will not be judged.)

Constructive criticism ought to consistently be a greeting, l a welcome and healthy gift whenever given in a spirit of love. In any case, we reserve no privilege to give devaluing or depreciating criticism of another, for that is attempting to be a judge over that person, and God alone is our appointed authority (God alone is THE JUDGE of all).

(Matthew 7:1 KJV)

PROMISE FROM GOD

"For he that in these things serveth Christ is acceptable to God, and approved of men."

If you serve Christ with this disposition (attitude), you will please God. What's more, other Christians will approve of you, also.

(Romans 14:18 KJV)

DEATH

73. What happens when one dies?

"But I would not have you to be ignorant, brethren, concerning them which are asleep, that ye sorrow not, even as others which have no hope."

"For if we believe that Jesus died and rose again, even so them also which sleep in Jesus will God bring with him."

"For this we say unto you by the word of the Lord, that we which are alive and remain unto the coming of the Lord shall not prevent them which are asleep."

"For the Lord himself shall descend from heaven with a shout, with the voice of the archangel, and with the trump of God; and the dead in Christ shall rise first:"

"Then we which are alive and remain shall be caught up together with them in the clouds, to meet the Lord in the air: and so shall we ever be with the Lord."

"Wherefore comfort one another with these words."

I want you to know what happens to Christians who have died.

(I Thessalonians 4:13-18 KJV)

"In a moment, in the twinkling of an eye, at the last trump: for the trumpet shall sound, and the dead shall be raised incorruptible, and we shall be changed."

When the trumpet sounds, those Christians who have died will be raised with changed bodies (transformed bodies).

(I Corinthians 15:52 KJV)

"And the third angel followed them, saying with a loud voice, If any man worship the beast and his image, and receive his mark in his forehead, or in his hand,"

"The same shall drink of the wine of the wrath of God, which he poured out without mixture into the cup of his indignation; and he shall be tormented with fire and brimstone in the presence of the holy angels, and in the presence of the Lamb:"

"And the smoke of their torment ascendeth up for ever and ever; and they have no rest day nor night, who worship the beast and his image, and whosoever receiveth the mark of his name."

"Here is the patience of the saints: here are they that keep the commandments of God, and the faith of Jesus."

Those who do not believe and accept Jesus Christ (Non-Christians) will have no relief day nor night, for they have worshiped the beast and his statue and have accepted the mark of his name.

(Revelation 14: 9-12) KJV

"And whosoever was not found written in the book of life was cast into the lake of fire."

(Revelation 20:15 KJV)

"And I heard a great voice out of heaven saying, Behold, the tabernacle of God is with men, and he will dwell with them, and they shall be his people, and God himself shall be with them, and be their God."

"And I heard a great voice out of heaven swaying, Behold, the tabernacle of God is with men, and he well dwell with them, and they shall be his people, and God himself shall be with them, and be their God."

A Christian who dies will meet God and live with him forever. An individual who is certainly not a Christian will be sentenced (condemned) to endless (eternal) punishment.

(Revelation 21:3 KJV)

74. How do I keep a proper perspective about death? Why am I so afraid of death?

"If ye then be risen with Christ, seek those things which are above, where Christ sitteth on the right hand of God."

"Set your affection on things above, not on things on the earth."

"For ye are dead, and your life is hid with Christ in God."

Since you have been raised to new existence (new life) with Christ, put your focus on the realities of heaven...Let heaven fill your thoughts...

(Colossians 3:1-3 KJV)

"For we know that if our earthly house of this tabernacle were dissolved, we have a building of God, and house not made with hands, eternal in the heavens."

"For in this we groan, earnestly desiring to be clothed upon with our house which is from heaven:"

"If so be that being clothed we shall not be found naked."

"For we that are in this tabernacle do groan, being burdened: not for that we would be unclothed, but clothed upon, that mortality might be swallowed up of life."

"Now he that hath wrought us for the selfsame thing is God, who also hath given unto us the earnest of the Spirit."

"Therefore we are always confident, knowing that, whilst we are at home in the body, we are absent from the Lord:"

"(For we walk by faith, not by sight:)"

"We are confident, I say, and willing rather to be absent from the body, and to be present with the Lord."

"Wherefore we labour, that, whether present or absent, we may be accepted of him."

"For we must all appear before the judgment seat of Christ; that every one may receive the things done in his body, according to that he hath done, whether it be good or bad."

(We want to slip into our new bodies so that these dying bodies will be swallowed up by everlasting life).

Fear of the unknown is natural, and fear of death can be healthy if it attracts us to know more about God.

It is useful to consider death a beginning, not an end. It is our passageway into eternal life with God.

(II Corinthians 5:1-10 KJV)

"For to me to live is Christ, and to die is gain."

A fear of death might be a sign of a frail relationship with God. You should be prepared to die (find a sense of contentment with yourself) so as to appreciate life completely (fully).

(Philippians 1:21 KJV)

"And if Christ be in you, the body is dead because of sin; but the Spirit is life because of righteousness."

When we accept Jesus Christ, we are given eternal life. This does not prevent the death of our body, but it does assure true life with him in heaven forever and ever. And is not that the life counts that counts the most?

(Romans 8:10 KJV)

75. In life after death, do we keep these bodies or do we receive new ones, or do we have no bodies at all?'

"So also is the resurrection of the dead. It is sown in corruption; it is raised in incorruption:"

Our earthly bodies, which die and decay, will be transformed to different bodies when they are resurrected, for they will never die.

Our present bodies become ill and become a burden for us. They age and decay. We wouldn't generally want to live in them until the end of time. Figure what number of issues we would gather in a couple thousand years! We will welcome the new bodies God gives us when we die and abandon these present bodies.

(I Corinthians 15:42 KJV)

PROMISES FROM GOD

"Jesus said unto her, I am the resurrection, and the life: he that believeth in me, though he were dead, yet shall he live:"

"And whosoever liveth and believeth in me shall never die. Believeth thou this?"

(John 11:25, 26 KJV)

DECEIT

76. How can I know when I'm being deceived?

"And De-li'-lah said to Samson, Tell me, I pray thee, wherein thy great strength lieth, and wherewith thou mightest be bound to afflict thee."

We are regularly deceived when we want to believe what we know we shouldn't. When our heart (our conscience) tells us no and our desires reveal to us truly a definite yes, we should listen to our conscience.

(Judges 16:6 KJV)

"All scripture is given by inspiration of God, and is profitable for doctrine, for reproof, for correction, for instruction in righteousness:"

All scripture is inspired by God and is useful to teach us what is true.

(II Timothy 3:16 KJV)

“These were more noble than those in Thes-sa-lo-ni’-ca, in that they received the word with all readiness of mind, and searched the scriptures daily, whether those things were so.”

(They searched the Scriptures day after day to check on Paul and Silas)

If somebody is attempting to persuade you to accomplish something that contradicts Scripture, you can be assured it isn’t right.

(Acts 17:11 KJV)

“And when the woman saw that the tree was good for food, and that it was pleasant to the eyes, and a tree to be desired to make one wise, she took of the fruit thereof, and did eat, and gave also unto her husband with her; and he did eat.”

(The fruit looked so fresh and delicious, and it would make her so wise!)

The promise of deception usually seems too good to be true.

(Genesis 3:6 KJV)

"Go from the presence of a foolish man, when thou perceivest not in him the lips of knowledge."

How frequently we overlook evident realities (truths) - avoid misleading individuals (deceitful people) in the event that you need to shield from being hoodwinked (deceived).

(Proverbs 14:7 KJV)

"But evil men and seducers shall wax worse and worse, deceiving, and being deceived."

For whatever length of time that Satan has capacity to deceive, he will trick (deceive) others, and they thus will attempt to deceive us. The most noticeably awful sort of deceiver is the false teacher, who seems to appear for our good, just to lead us on a dangerous way (a destructive path).

(II Timothy 3:13 KJV)

77. How do we deceive ourselves?

"The heart is deceitful above all things, and desperately wicked; who can know it?

Yes, the human heart is most deceitful!

(Jeremiah 17:9 KJV)

"Be not deceived; God is not mocked: for whosoever a man soweth, that shall he also reap."

Be not misled. Remember that you can't ignore God and get away with sin. We deceive ourselves when we think we can ignore God and still receive his blessings.

(Galatians 6:7 KJV)

"Let no man deceive himself. If any man among you seemeth to be wise in this world, let him become a fool, that he may be wise."

Quit tricking yourselves. If you think you are savvy (wise) by this current world's measures, you should turn into a nitwit (fool) so you can become wise by God's standards.

We deceive ourselves when we live as if this world is everything or the only thing that matters.

(I Corinthians 3:18 KJV)

PROMISE FROM GOD

"Whereforth putting away lying, NEIGHBOUR: for we are members one of another."

Put away all falsehood and "tell your neighbor the truth," because we belong to each other.

(Ephesians 4:25 KJV)

DECISIONS

78. What are some principles of good decision making?

"He that answereth a matter before he heareth it, it is folly and shame unto him."

Have all the facts before you answering and giving advice.

(Proverbs 18:13 KJV)

"The heart of the prudent getteth knowledge; and the ear of the wise seeketh knowledge."

Intelligent people are always open to new ideas. In fact, they look for them. Be open to ideas.

(Proverbs 18:15 KJV)

"And this is the confidence that we have in him, that, if we ask any thing according to his will, he heareth us:"

God listens to us when we are confident that he does and ask anything according to his will; so seek God's guidance.

(I John 5:14 KJV)

"The way of a fool is right in his own eyes: but he that hearkeneth unto counsel is wise."

Often time fools think they need no advice, but the wise listen to others. Seek the advice of trusted friends.

(Proverbs 12:15 KJV)

"Thou through my commandments hast made me wiser than mine enemies: for they are ever with me."

Be certain that your decisions are not based on values that contradict God's word.

(Psalm 119:98 KJV)

"Shew me thy ways, O LORD; teach me thy paths."

Lord, order my steps on the right road for me to follow.

Knowing the scriptures and gathering their insight (wisdom) give us more alternatives in our dynamic and give us the discernment we have to settle on healthy options.

A right decision is one that is consistent with the principles of truth found in God's Word. If just one of the alternatives would please God, that is the correct choice/decision.

If there are a several options that are consistent with God's Word, at that point as opposed to the decision itself, the most significant thing might be the process of believing and trusting God to assist you with taking advantage of the way you choose/ or decide.

(Psalm 25:4 KJV)

79. How do I know if I have made a good decision?

"Help us, O God of our salvation, for the glory of thy name: and deliver us, and purge away our sins, for thy name's sake."

Your decision is a good decision when what you've decided honors God.

(Psalm 79:9 KJV)

"But the fruit of the Spirit is love, joy, peace, longsuffering, gentleness, goodness, faith,"

"Meekness, temperance: against such there is no law."

When the fruits of the Spirit produce good results you know you've made a good decision.

(Galatians 5:22, 23 KJV)

"But strong meat belongeth to them that are of full age, even those who by reason of use have their senses exercised to discern both good and evil."

You will reliably use sound judgment if you are investing steady energy in God's Word and following up on its principles.

(Hebrews 5:14 KJV)

"And we know that all things work together for good to them that love God, to them who are called according to his purpose."

We know God causes everything to work together for the good of those who love him and are called by him.

Regardless of whether we don't generally settle on the best choice/decision, God has the ability to settle on the choice turn out to our greatest advantage (our best interests, according to his purpose).

(Romans 8:28 KJV)

80. Should I put out a "fleece"?

"And Gideon said unto God, Let not thine anger be hot against me, and I will speak but this once; let me prove, I pray thee, but this once with the fleece; let it now be dry only upon the fleece, and upon all the ground let there be dew."

Gideon's model is frequently used by Christians confronting a decision. Nonetheless, great caution must be practiced when putting out a fleece, s because it tends to limit the options of a God who has unlimited options available to us.

(Judges 6:39 KJV)

PROMISE FROM GOD

"In all thy ways acknowledge him, and he shall direct thy paths."

(Seek his will in everything (all) you do, and he will direct thy paths).

(Proverbs 3:6 KJV)

DEPRESSION

81. Does God care when I feel depressed?

"O LORD, thou hast searched me, and known me."

"Thou knowest my downsitting and mine uprising, thou understandest my thought afar

off."

"Thou compassest my path and my lying down, and art acquainted with all my ways."

"For there is not a word in my tongue, but, lo, O LORD, thou knowest it altogether."

"Thou hast beset me behind and before, and laid thine hand upon me."

"Such knowledge is too wonderful for me; it is high, I cannot attain unto it."

"Whither shall I go from thy spirit? Or whither shall I flee from thy presence?

"If I ascend up into heaven, thou art there: if I make my bed in hell, behold, thou art there."

"If I take the wings of the morning, and dwell in the uttermost parts of the sea;"

"Even there shall thy hand lead me, and thy right hand shall hold me."

"If I say, Surely the darkness shall cover me; even the night shall be light about me."

"Yea, the darkness hideth not from thee; but the night shineth as the day: the darkness and the light are both alike to thee."

There is no depth to which we can descend that God is not present with us. At the point when wretchedness comes, we should recall that despite the fact that we can't see or feel his presence, he has not abandoned us.

(Psalm 139:1-12 KJV)

"Out of the depths have I cried unto thee, O LORD."

"Lord, hear my voice: let thine ears be attentive to the voice of my supplications."

"If thou, LORD, shouldest mark iniquities, O Lord, who shall stand?"

"But there is forgiveness with thee, that thou mayest be feared."

"I wait for the LORD, my soul doth wait, and in his word do I hope."

"My soul waiteth for the Lord more than they that watch for the morning: I say, more than they that watch for the morning."

"Let Israel hope in the LORD: for with the LORD there is mercy, and with him is plenteous redemption."

"And he shall redeem Israel from all his iniquities."

We cry out to God in prayer even from the darkest night of despair. God will hear us.

(Psalm 130:1-8 KJV)

"He is despised and rejected of men; a man of sorrows, and acquainted with grief: and we hid as it were our faces from him; he was despised, and we esteemed him not."

We know that through Jesus Christ God understands the pain of human life.

(Isaiah 53:3 KJV)

"Nor height, nor depth, nor any other creature, shall be able to separate us from the love of God, which is in Christ Jesus our Lord."

Nothing can separate us from the love of God – not even life's worst depression can separate us from the love of Christ.

(Romans 8:39 KJV)

82. Does feeling depressed mean something is wrong with my faith?

"And he was sore athirst, and called on the LORD, and said Thou hast given this great deliverance into the hand of thy servant: and now shall I die for thirst, and fall into the hand of the uncircumcised?"

(Now Samson was very thirsty, and he cried out to the LORD, "You have accomplished this great victory... Must I now die of thirst?)"

(Judges 15:18 KJV)

"And when he saw that, he arose, and went for his life, and came to Be'-er-she'-ba, which belongeth to Judah, and left his servant there."

"But he himself went a day's journey into the wilderness, and came and sat down under a juniper tree: and he requested for himself that he might die; and said, It is enough; now, O LORD, take away my life; for I am not better than my fathers."

Depression can often follow spiritual victory or great achievement, even for God's people.

(I Kings 19:3,4 KJV)

"And my soul shall be joyful in the LORD: it shall rejoice in his salvation."

I am glad because it is God who rescues me.

(Psalm 35:9 KJV)

"I waited patiently for the LORD; and he inclined unto me, and heard my cry."

"He brought me up also out of an horrible pit, out of the miry clay, and set my feet upon a rock, and established my goings."

"And he hath put a new song in my mouth, even praise unto our God: many shall see it, and fear, and shall trust in the LORD."

God lifted me out of the pit of despair...

(Psalm 40:1-3 KJV)

"And he said, Come. And when Peter was come down out of the ship, he walked on the water, to go to Jesus."

"But when he saw the wind boisterous, he was afraid; and beginning to sink, he cried, saying, Lord, save me."

"And immediately Jesus stretched forth his hand, and caught him, and said unto him, O thou of little faith, wherefore didst thou doubt?"

God is able to lift us out of the pit of depression and fear.

(Matthew 14:29-31 KJV)

PROMISE FROM GOD

"Come unto me, all ye that labour and are heavy laden, and I will give you rest."

"Take my yoke upon you, and learn of me; for I am meek and lowly in heart: and ye shall find rest unto your souls."

"For my yoke is easy, and my burden is light."

Then Jesus said, "Come to me, every one of you who are tired and worry about overwhelming concerns, and I will give you rest. Take my burden upon you. Let me show you, since I am modest and delicate, and you will discover rest for your souls. For my yoke fits superbly, and the burden I give you is light."

(Matthew 11:28-30 KJV)

DESIRES

83. Is it OK to want something?

"In Gib'-e-on the LORD appeared to Solomon in a dream by night: and God said, Ask what I shall give thee."

God said, "What do you want? Ask, and I will give it to you!"

(I Kings 3:5 KJV)

"Hope deferred maketh the heart sick, but when the desire cometh, it is a tree of life."

Hope deferred makes the heart wiped sick, however when dreams work out as expected, there is life and happiness (joy).

God made desire within us as a methods for communicating. Desire is acceptable and sound whenever coordinated toward the best possible object of desire; what is acceptable and right and God-fearing (God-respecting, God- honoring).

(Proverbs 13:12 KJV)

"Whom have I in heaven but thee? And there is none upon earth that I desire beside thee."

I desire you Lord more than anything on earth!

(Psalm 73:25 KJV)

"Yea, in the way of thy judgments, O LORD, have we waited for thee; the desire of our soul is to thy name, and to the remembrance of thee."

LORD, We love to obey your laws; our heart's desire is to glorify your name.

(Isaiah 26:8 KJV)

"Finally, brethren, whatsoever things are true, whatsoever things are honest, whatsoever things are just, whatsoever things are pure, whatsoever things are lovely, whatsoever things are of good report; if there be any virtue, and if there be any praise, think on these things."

Fix your thoughts on what is true and honorable and right. Consider things that are pure and lovely and splendid (admirable).

Desiring sin is never right. Ensure the object of your longing (desire) is acceptable, consistent with God's Word, and not unsafe (harmful) to other people.

(Philippians 4:8 KJV)

84. How do I resist evil desires?

"Who is a wise man and endued with knowledge among you? Let him shew out of a good conversation his works with meekness of wisdom."

Carry on with a life of consistent goodness so just great deeds will pour forward.

Keep yourself occupied.

(James 3:13 KJV)

"And lead us not into temptation, but deliver us from evil: For thine is the kingdom, and the power, and the glory, for ever. A-men."

Lord, let us not yield to temptation, but rather deliver us from the evil one. Pray about it.

(Matthew 6:13 KJV)

"And Jo-si'-ah took away all the abominations out of all the countries that pertained to the children of Israel, and made all that were present in Israel to serve, even to serve the LORD their God. And all his days they departed not from following the LORD, the God of their fathers."

Here, Josiah removed all detestable idols. Take away the source of temptation.

(II Chronicles 34:33 KJV)

"Set your affection on things above, not on things on the earth."

Let heaven fill your thoughts. Fill your mind with God.

(Colossians 3:2 KJV)

"Without counsel purposes are disappointed: but in the multitude of counsellors they are established."

Plans go wrong for lack of advice; many counselors bring success.

(Proverbs 15:22 KJV)

85. Can God help me change the desires within my heart?

"For when we were in the flesh, the motions of sins, which were by the law, did work in our members to bring forth fruit unto death."

"But now we are delivered from the law, that being dead wherein we were held; that we should serve in newness of spirit, and not in the oldness of the letter."

Now we can really serve God, not by the law but by the new way, by the Spirit."

(Romans 7:5, 6 KJV)

"Then rose up the chief of the fathers of Judah and Benjamin, and the priests, and the Levites, with all them whose spirit God had raised, to go up to build the house of the LORD which is in Jerusalem."

God stirs our hearts with right desires. It is up to us to act on them.

(Ezra 1:5 KJV)

PROMISE FROM GOD

"A new heart also will I give you, and a new spirit will I put within you: and I will take away the stony heart out of your flesh, and I will give you an heart of flesh."

What's more, I will give you a new heart with new and right desires, and I will place a new spirit in you. I will take out your stony hearts of transgression and give you new devoted, obedient hearts.

(Ezekiel 36:26 KJV)

DIVORCE

86. What are some ways to prevent divorce?

"Therefore as the church is subject unto Christ, so let the wives be to their own husbands in every thing."

"Husbands. Love your wives, even as Christ also loved the church, and gave himself for it;"

(Ephesians 5:24, 25 KJV)

"Wherefore comfort yourselves together, and edify one another, even as also ye do."

Encourage each other and build each other up.

Couples who love each other with the kind of love Christ showed when he died for us, and who seek to please one another, and who encourage one another and develop each other - these are the couples who will probably stay together in a happy marriage. The configuration is basic, however the fulfillment takes some doing! Never let your marriage become a marriage of accommodation (convenience).

(I Thessalonians 5:11 KJV)

87. How do I handle bitterness I feel from divorce?

"Looking diligently lest any man fall of the grace of God; lest any man fail of the grace of God; lest any root of bitterness springing up trouble you, and thereby many be defiled;"

If you are a casualty (victim) of divorce, you may have been hurt badly, you may have been dealt with shamefully (unjustly), you may have been humiliated. Be that as it may, if you permit your bitterness to fester and develop, it will dominate everything you do and render you useless for effectively serving God. You should release your bitterness (let it go) and forgive, with the goal that God's Holy Spirit can keep on working in your life and help you with starting over again.

(Hebrews 12:15 KJV)

88. If I get divorced will God forgive me?

"Who forgiveth all thine iniquities; who healeth all thy diseases;"

God forgives all my sins.

(Psalm 103:3 KJV)

"If we confess our sins, he is faithful and just to forgive us our sins, and to cleanse us from all unrighteousness."

No sin is past God's forgiveness, and nothing others do against us can isolate us from God's unlimited love.

Regardless of what befalls you, let God reestablish (restore) you to wholeness.

(I John 1:9 KJV)

89. What the Bible say about divorce?

"Yet ye say, Wherefore? Because the LORD hath been witness between thee and the wife of thy youth, against whom thou hast dealt treacherously: yet is she thy companion, and the wife of thy covenant."

"And did not he make one? Yet had he the residue of the spirit. And wherefore one? That he might seek a godly seed. Therefore take heed to your spirit, and let none deal treacherously against the wife of his youth."

"For the LORD, the God of Israel, saith that he hateth putting away: for one covereth violence with his garment, saith the LORD of hosts: therefore take heed to your spirit, that ye deal not treacherously."

You cry out, "Why has the LORD abandoned us?" I'll tell you why! Because the LORD witnessed the vows you and your wife made to each other on your wedding day...But you have been disloyal...Didn't the LORD make you one..." In body and spirit are his... So guard yourself; remain loyal... "For I hate divorce!" says the LORD...

God considers divorce to be off-base (wrong) because it is the breaking of a coupling responsibility (a binding commitment). One or the two life partners (one or both spouses) have settled on a conscious decision to be unfaithful.

(Malachi 2:14-16 KJV)

"The Pharisees also came unto him, tempting him, and saying unto him, Is it lawful for a man to put away his wife for every cause?"

"And he answered and said unto them, Have ye not read, that he which made them at the beginning MADE THEM MALE AND FEMALE,"

"And said, FOR THIS CAUSE SHALL A MAN LEAVE FATHER AND MOTHER, AND SHALL CLEAVE TO HIS WIFE: AND THEY TWAIN SHALL BE ONE FLESH?"

Wherefore they are no more twain, but one flesh. What therefore God hath joined together, let not man put asunder."

"They say unto him, Why did Moses then command to give a writing of divorcement, and to put her away?"

"He saith unto them, Moses because of the hardness of your hearts suffered you to put away your wives: but from the beginning it was not so."

"And I say unto you, Whosoever shall put away his wife, except it be for fornication, and shall marry another, committeth adultery: and whoso marrieth her which is put away doth commit adultery."

There is a wide scope of interpretation concerning this passage, with wide application to explicit circumstances. The Old Testament accommodated explicit guidelines concerning divorce and limited remarriage in special cases (see Deuteronomy 24:1-4), while simultaneously clarifying that divorce isn't God's intention (Malachi 2:14-16).

The New Testament makes it clear that divorce is wrong (Matthew 5:31, 32; I Corinthians 7:10,11), while allowing for limited exceptions as Jesus mentions in this passage.

(Matthew 19:3-9 KJV)

PROMISE FROM GOD

"May be able to comprehend with all saints what is the breadth, and length, and depth, and height;"

And may you have the power to understand … how wide, how long, how high, and how deep his love really is.

(Ephesians 3:18 KJV)

90. Is it OK to doubt my faith?

"When your fathers tempted me, proved me, and saw my work."

"For there your ancestors tried my patience; they courted my wrath though they had seen my many miracles."

God gives us a lot of proof (evidence) to have faith in him. Doubt comes when we neglect to stop sufficiently long enough to observe all the evidence. What's more, when uncertainty (doubt) turns to lack of trust, we are at risk of ignoring God altogether.

(Psalm 95:9 KJV)

"Then saith he to Thomas, Reach hither thy finger, and behold my hands; and reach hither thy hand, and thrust it into my side: and be not faithless, but believing."

"And Thomas answered and said unto him, My Lord and my God."

"Jesus saith unto him, Thomas, because thou hast seen me, thou hast believed: bless are they that have not seen, and yet have believed."

Doubt can be healthy or destructive, depending on how we use it.

"Don't be faithless any longer. Believe!"

(John 20:27-29 KJV)

"And the serpent said unto the woman, Ye shall not surely die:"

"For God doth know that in the day ye eat thereof, then your eyes shall be opened, and ye shall be as gods, knowing good and evil."

"And when the woman saw that the tree was good for food, and that it was pleasant to the eyes, and a tree to be desire to make one wise, she took of the fruit thereof, and did eat, and gave also unto her husband with her; and he did eat."

"You won't die!" the serpent hissed..."

One of Satan's strategies is to get us to question God's integrity (God's goodness). He attempts to get us to overlook all God has given us and spotlight on what we don't have. If you are investing quite a bit of your energy and time pondering what you don't have, you might be slipping into unfortunate uncertainty (destructive, unhealthy doubt).

(Genesis 3:4-6 KJV)

91. Are there things we should never doubt?

"Which is the earnest of our inheritance until the redemption of the purchased possession, unto the praise of his glory."

"The Spirit is God's guarantee that he will give us everything he promised and that he has purchased us to be his own people."

(Ephesians 1:14 KJV)

"Let your conversation be without covetousness; and be content with such things as ye have: for he hath said, I WILL NEVER LEAVE THEE, NOR FORSAKE THEE."

We should never doubt our salvation. Once we become Christians, Satan can never snatch us away.

(Hebrews 13:5 KJV)

"(For he saith, I HAVE HEARD THEE IN A TIME ACCEPTED, AND IN THE DAY OF SALVATION HAVE I SUCCOURED THEE: behold, now is the accepted time; behold, now is the day of salvation.)"

God is ready to help you right now.

We should never doubt God's desire or ability to help us.

(II Corinthians 6:2 KJV)

PROMISE FROM GOD

"For verily I say unto you, That whosoever shall say unto this mountain, Be thou removed, and be thou cast into the sea; and shall not doubt in his heart, but shall believe that those things which he saith shall come to pass; he shall have whatsoever he saith."

I assure you that you can say to this mountain, "May God lift you up and toss you into the ocean," and your command will be complied. All that is required is that you truly believe and don't question (don't doubt) in your heart.

(Mark 11:23 KJV)

ENCOURAGEMENT

92. How can I encourage others?

"Then the prophets, Hag'-gai the prophet, and Zech-a-ri'-ah the son of Id'-do, prophesied unto the Jews that were in Judah and Jerusalem in the name of the God of Israel, even unto them."

"Then rose up Ze-rub'-ba-bel the son of She-al'-ti-el, and Jesh'-u-a the son of Joz'-a-dak, and began to build the house of God which is at Jerusalem: and with them were the prophets of God helping them."

Encouragement sometimes means getting a person involved once again in productive work.

(Ezra 5:1, 2 KJV)

"Who, when he came, and had seen the grace of God, was glad, and exhorted them all, that with purpose of heart they would cleave unto the Lord."

(Barnabas) encouraged the believers to stay true to the Lord.

Barnabas is known as the "great encourager" in the Bible Barnabas' consolation (encouragement) of John Mark helped him become an extraordinary innovator (great leader) in the church. Encouragement is more than empty applause; it is encouraging others to hold fast to the principles of faith.

(Acts 11:23 KJV)

"Which in time past was to thee unprofitable, but now profitable to thee and to me:"

Showing trust in a person is a great source of encouragement to him or her.

(Philemon 1:11 KJV)

"Who, being in the form of God, thought it not robbery to be equal with God:"

"And I am sure that God, who began the good work within you, will continue his work until it is finally finished.

Encouragement is affirming others and the work they are doing for God.

(Philippians 1:6 KJV)

"And Joshua said unto all the people. Thus saith the LORD God of Israel, Your fathers dwelt on the other side of the flood in old time, even Te'-rah, the father of Abraham, and the father of Na'-chor: and they served other gods."

"And I took your father Abraham from the other side of the flood, and led him throughout all the land of Canaan, and multiplied his seed, and gave him Isaac."

"And I gave unto Isaac Jacob and Esau; and I gave unto Esau mount Se'-ir, to possess it; but Jacob and his children went down into Egypt."

"I sent Moses also and Aaron, and I plagued Egypt, according to that which I did among them: and afterward I brought you out."

"And I brought your fathers out of Egypt: and came unto the sea; and the Egyptians pursued after your fathers with chariots and horsemen unto the Red sea."

"And when they cried unto the LORD, he put darkness between you and the Egyptians, and brought the sea upon them, and covered them; and your eyes have seen what I have done in Egypt: and ye dwelt in the wilderness a long season."

"And I brought you into the land of the Am'-or-ites, which dwelt on the other side Jordan; and they fought with you: and I gave them into your hand, that ye might possess their land; and I destroyed them from before you."

"Then Ba'-lak the son of Zip'-por, king of Moab, arose and warred against Israel, and sent and called Ba'-laam the son of Be'-or to curse you:"

"But I would not hearken unto Ba'-laam; therefore he blessed you still: so I delivered you out of his hand."

"And ye went over Jordan, and came unto Jericho: and the men of Jericho fought against you, the Am'-or-ites, and the Per'-iz-zites, and the Ca'-naan-ites, and the Hit'-tites, and the Gir'-ga-shites, the Hi'-vites, and the Jeb'-u-sites; and I delivered them into your hand."

"And I sent the hornet before you, which drave them out from before you, even the two kings of the Am'-or-ites; but not with thy sword, nor with thy bow."

"And I have given you a land for which ye did not labour, and cities which ye built not, and ye dwell in them; of the vineyards and oliveyards which ye planted not do ye eat."

"I gave you land you had not worked for, and I gave you cities you did not build..."

Encouragement can come from reviewing God's past blessings.

(Joshua 24:2-13 KJV)

"If I laughed on them, they believed it not; and the light of my countenance they cast not down."

At the point when they were disheartened, I smiled at them. My look of approval was precious to them.

In some cases only a grin or a smile is an extraordinary support (great encouragement).

(Job 29:24 KJV)

93. How do I handle discouragement?

"Be sober, be vigilant; because your adversary the devil, as a roaring lion, walketh about, seeking whom he may devour:"

"Whom resist stedfast in the faith, knowing that the same afflictions are accomplished in your brethren that are in the world."

"Be careful! Watch out for the attacks from the Devil, your great enemy. He lurks around like a thundering (roaring) lion, searching for some unfortunate casualty to devour. Take a firm stand against him, and be strong in your faith. Remember that Christians everywhere throughout the world are experiencing a similar kind of suffering you are."

Suffering produces demoralization (discouragement). At the point when we are discouraged we are especially helpless against Satan's attacks. We should be particularly mindful so as to stand close to God's Word and other believers during these troublesome (difficult) times.

(I Peter 5:8, 9 KJV)

"But as for me, my feet were almost gone; my steps had well nigh slipped."

"For I was envious at the foolish, when I saw the prosperity of the wicked."

Often times we become disheartened (discouraged) when we stop looking at all God has given us and spotlight on the accomplishment of others.

(Psalm 73:2, 3 KJV)

"And he said, Hearken ye, all Judah, and ye inhabitants of Jerusalem, and thou king Je-hosh'-a-phat, Thus saith the LORD unto you, Be not afraid nor dismayed by reason of this great multitude; for the battle is not your's, but God's."

"To morrow go ye down against them: behold, they come up by the cliff of Ziz; and ye shall find them at the end of the brook, before the wilderness of Je-ru'-el."

"Ye shall not need to fight in this battle: set yourselves, stand ye still, and see the salvation of the LORD with you, O Judah and Jerusalem: fear not, nor be dismayed; tomorrow go out against them: for the LORD will be with you."

It would have been simple for the people of Judah to see just the tremendous enemy army, and not God standing over it to annihilate it. We should be mindful so as to separate our sentiments of demoralization (discouragement) from our assurance of God's love for us.

Discouragement can cause us to question (doubt) God's love, drawing us away from the wellspring (source) of our greatest help.

(II Chronicles 20:15-17 KJV)

PROMISE FROM GOD

"Now our Lord Jesus Christ himself, and God, even our Father, which hath loved us, and hath given us everlasting consolation and good hope through grace,"

"Comfort your hearts, and stablish you in every good word and work."

(II Thessalonians 2:16, 17 KJV)

ENVIRONMENT

94. What does the Bible say about the environment and our responsibility in environmental issues?

"And God said, Let us make man in our image, after our likeness: and let them have dominion over the fish of the sea, and over the fowl of the air, and over the cattle, and over all the earth, and over every creeping thing that creepeth upon the earth."

"So God created man in his own image, in the image of God created he him; male and female created he them."

"And God blessed them, and God said unto them, Be fruitful, and multiply, and replenish the earth, and subdue it: and have dominion over the fish of the sea, and over the fowl of the air, and over every living thing that moveth upon the earth."

"And God said, Behold, I have given you every herb bearing seed, which is upon the face of all the earth, and every tree, in the which is the fruit of a tree yielding seed; to you it shall be for meat."

"And to every beast of the earth, and to every fowl of the air, and to every thing that creepeth upon the earth, wherein is life, I have given every green herb for meat; and it was so."

God created man (human beings) to share responsibility regarding the earth by being acceptable (good) stewards of the created environment.

(Genesis 1:26-30 KJV)

"And the LORD God took the man, and put him into the garden of Eden to dress it and to keep it."

The first assignment God gave to Adam was to tend and care for the Garden of Eden.

(Genesis 2:15 KJV)

"When thou shalt besiege a city a long time, in making war against it to take it, thou shalt not destroy the trees thereof by forcing an ax against them: for thou mayest eat of them, and thou shalt not cut them down (for the tree of the field is man's life) to employ them in the siege:"

"Only the trees which thou knowest that they be not trees for meat, thou shalt destroy and cut them down; and thou shalt build bulwarks against the city that maketh war with thee, until it be subdued."

Even in the time of war God was concerned about the needless destruction of the environment.

(Deuteronomy 20:19, 20 KJV)

"AND the LORD spake unto Moses in mount Si'-nai, saying,"

"Speak unto the children of Israel, and say unto them, When ye come into the land which I give you, then shall the land keep a sabbath unto the LORD."

"Six years thou shalt sow thy field, and six years thou shall prune thy vineyard, and gather in the fruit thereof;"

"But in the seventh year shall be a sabbath of rest unto the land, a sabbath for the LORD: thou shalt neither sow thy field, nor prune thy vineyard."

"That which groweth of its own accord of thy harvest thou shalt not reap, neither gather the grapes of thy vine undressed: for it is a year of rest unto the land."

"And the sabbath of the land shall be meat for you; for thee, and for thy servant, and for thy maid, and for thy hired servant, and for thy stranger that sojourneth with thee,"

"And for thy cattle, and for the beast that are in thy land, shall all the increase thereof be meat."

God's instructions for the people of Israel to let the farmland rest each seventh year considered the preservation of good, beneficial (productive) land.

(Leviticus 25:1-7 KJV)

"Let the heavens rejoice, and let the earth be glad; let the sea roar, and the fulness thereof."

"Let the field be joyful, and all that is therein: then shall all the trees of the wood rejoice"

"Before the LORD: for he cometh, for he cometh to judge the earth: he shall judge the world with righteousness, and the people with his truth."

Since God's glory is unmistakably found in the magnificence of nature, the earth ought to never be negligently, thoughtlessly defiled.

(Psalm 96:11-13 KJV)

PROMISE FROM GOD

"Behold the fowls of the air: for they sow not, neither do they reap, nor gather into barns; yet your heavenly Father feedeth them. Are ye not much better than they?"

"Which of you by taking thought can add one cubit unto his stature?"

"And why take ye thought for raiment? Consider the lilies of the field, how they grow; they toil not, neither do thy spin:"

"And yet I say unto you, That even Solomon in all his glory was not arrayed like one of these."

"Wherefore, if God so clothe the grass of the field, which to day is, and to morrow is cast into the oven, shall he not much more clothe you, O ye of little faith?"

Take a look at the winged birds. They don't have to plant or collect or put nourishment in outbuildings on the grounds that your heavenly Father takes care of them. Also, you are unquestionably more significant to him than they are. Could every one of your stresses (worries) add a solitary minute to your life? Obviously not. Furthermore, why stress over your garments? Take a look at the lilies and how they grow. They don't work or make their apparel, yet Solomon in all his glory was not dressed as beautifully as they seem to be. What's more, God cares about flowers that are here today and gone tomorrow, won't he all the more without a doubt more surely care for you?

(Matthew 6:26-30 KJV)

EXAMPLE

95. Which examples (role models) are to be followed and which examples to be avoided?

"Thou shalt not bow down to their gods, nor serve them, nor do after their works; but thou shalt utterly overthrow them, and quite break down their images."

"Do not to worship the gods of these other nations... and never follow their evil model (evil example)."

Each individual on earth is an example (role model) of something to somebody. We follow examples, and we as a whole set an example for other people.

Our personal presence not just impacts others in issues of day by day living, but additionally for good or evil, Christ or Satan. What kind of role model or example have you been displaying lately to other people?

(Exodus 23:24 KJV)

"For a bishop must be blameless, as the steward of God; not self-willed, not soon angry, not given to wine, no striker, not given to filthy lucre;"

"And you yourself must be an example to them by carrying out beneficial things (Good deeds) of every sort."

Strive to be the sort of example people will want to follow.

(Titus 2:7 KJV)

96. Who is the ultimate role model?

"Be ye followers of me, even as I also am of Christ."

In others, we find grouped qualities we might want to follow. In Jesus Christ, we discover the entirety of the attributes we might want to follow. At the point when you have an inquiry about what to do, ask what Jesus would have done.

(I Corinthians 11:1 KJV)

97. How can I be a good example?

"Knowing, brethren beloved, your election of God."

"For our gospel came not unto you in word only, but also in power, and in the Holy Ghost, and in much assurance; as ye know what manner of men we were among you for your sake."

"And ye became followers of us, and of the Lord, have received the word in much affliction, with joy of the Holy Ghost:"

A good role model is responsible and accountable.

(I Thessalonians 1:4-6 KJV)

"See, I have this day set thee over the nations and over the kingdoms, to root out, and to pull down, and to destroy, and to throw down, to build, and to plant."

A good role model does not only do what is right but speaks out against wrong.

(Jeremiah 1:10 KJV)

"For when for the time ye ought to be teachers, ye have need that one teach you again which be the first principles of the oracles of God; and are become such as have need of milk, and not of strong meat."

A good role model teaches others about God's ways.

(Hebrews 5:12 KJV)

"Let no man despise thy youth; but be thou an example of the believers, in word, in conversation, in charity, in spirit, in faith, in purity."

One's age has nothing to do with being a good role model, set the example.

(I Timothy 4:12 KJV)

"Ye are the salt of the earth: but if the salt have lost his savour, wherewith shall it be salted? It is thenceforth good for nothing, but to be cast out, and to be trodden under foot of men."

A good role model influences others to do good rather than being easily influenced by evil.

(Matthew 5:13 KJV)

"Then shall we know, if we follow on to know the LORD: his going forth is prepared as the morning; and he shall come unto us as the rain, as the latter and former rain unto the earth."

A good role model is not a person who is perfect (only God is perfect), but that you are striving for maturity.

(Hosea 6:3 KJV)

"Even as the Son of man came not to be ministered unto, but to minister, and to give his life a ransom for many."

A good role model does not make you a celebrity; it makers you a servant.

(Matthew 20:28 KJV)

PROMISE FROM GOD

"Wherefore lift up the hands which hang down, and the feeble knees;"

"And make straight paths for your feet, lest that which is lame be turned out of the way; but let it rather be healed."

So take another hold with your tired hands and stand firm on your temperamental (shaky) legs. Mark out a straight path for your feet. At that point the individuals who follow you, though they are weak and lame, won't falter (stumble) and fall, but will become strong.

(Hebrews 12:12, 13 KJV)

EXCELLENCE

98. Where did excellence of workmanship have its origin?

"And God saw everything that he had made, and behold, it was very good. And the evening and the morning were the sixth day."

The splendor of immaculate creation was excellence in its most flawless form. In addition to the fact that it was excellent, it was excellent inside and out. The glory of the Creator (God) was reflected in the glory of his creation. That is the highest standard of excellence.

(Genesis 1:31 KJV)

"It shall blossom abundantly, and rejoice even with joy and singing: the glory of Leb'-a-non shall be given unto it, the excellency of Carmel and Shar'-on, they shall see the glory of the LORD, and the excellency of our God."

All nature sings and shows a beauty of symmetry that surpasses, that outperforms the best melodic, lovely, or aesthetic virtuoso (artistic genius) of all people together.

(Isaiah 35:2 KJV)

99. Why is excellence encouraged by God? Why should we strive to be excellent?

"And he hath filled him with the spirit of God, in wisdom, in understanding, and in knowledge, and in all manner of workmanship;"

"And to devise curious works, to work in gold, and in silver, and in brass,"

"And in the cutting of stones, to set them, and in carving of wood, to make any manner of cunning work."

"And he hath put in his heart that he may teach, both he, and A'ho'-li-ab, the son of A-his'-a-mach, of the tribe of Dan."

"Them hath he filled with wisdom of heart, to work all manner of work, of the engraver, and of the cunning workman, and of the embroiderer, in blue, and in purple, in scarlet, and in fine linen, and of the weaver, even of them that do any work, and of those that devise cunning work."

God places incredible incentive (great value) on excellence and imparts exceptional blessings in every one of us to help us become especially excellent in certain areas.

(Exodus 35:31-35 KJV)

"Also unto She-ma'-iah his son were sons born, that ruled throughout the house of their father: for they were mighty men of valour."

God places incredible incentive (great value) on excellence and imparts exceptional blessings in every one of us to help us become especially excellent in certain areas.

(I Chronicles 26:6 KJV)

"And the children of Israel that were present at Jerusalem kept the feast of unleavened bread seven days with great gladness; and the Levites and the priests praised the LORD day by day, singing with loud instruments unto the LORD."

"And Hez-e-ki'-ah spake comfortably unto all the Levites that taught the good knowledge of the LORD; and they did eat throughout the feast seven days, offering peace offerings, and making confession to the LORD God of their fathers."

Excellence is appreciated and it also inspires us.

(II Chronicles 30:21, 22 KJV)

"And I made treasures over the treasuries, Shel-e-mi'-ah the priest, and Za'-dok the scribe, and of the Levites, Pe-da'-iah: and next to them was Ha'-nan the son of Zac'-cur, the son of Mat-ta-ni'-ah: for they were counted faithful, and their office was to distribute unto their brethren."

These men has an excellent reputation, and it was their business (job) to make legitimate circulations (honest distributions) to their kindred Levites.

Excellence is identified with reputation. It makes you a decent good example (a good role model). Would you like to be known as an unremarkable (mediocre) person? Did God want to be known as a mediocre God?

(Nehemiah 13:13 KJV)

"And he gave some, apostles; and some, prophets; and some, evangelists; and some, pastors and teachers;"

"For the perfecting of the saints, for the work of the ministry, for the edifying of the body of Christ:"

God gave these gifts to equip his people to do his work and build up the church.

Excellence engages and challenges us. It urges us to make an extraordinary commitment, (a unique contribution).

(Ephesians 4:11, 12 KJV)

"If any man speak, let him speak as the oracles of God; if any man minister, let him do it as of the ability which God giveth: that God in all things may be glorified through Jesus Christ, to whom be praise and dominion for ever and ever. A-men'."

Are you called to help others? Do it with all the strength and energy that God supplies.

Excellent works are helpful to other people. For instance, specialists (doctors) who have strived for excellence in clinical research have created antibodies that have spared innumerable lives.

(I Peter 4:1 KJV 1)

"Sing unto the LORD with the harp; with the harp, and the voice of a psalm."

Excellence is an act of worship.

(Psalm 98:5 KJV)

"I therefore so run, not as uncertainly; so fight I, not as one that beateth the air:"

Excellence is an indication that we are striving to be like Christ, who was excellent in every way.

(I Corinthians 9:26 KJV)

100. What kind of life is more excellent than any other?

"But covet earnestly the best gifts: and yet shew I unto you a more excellent way."

The "more excellent way" articulation presents the incredible love chapter of the Bible - I Corinthians 13. Of everything on earth, love likely could be the most amazing, the most excellent. A life of love for God and each other is an existence of excellence that is really glorious (majestic) and amazingly awesome.

(I Corinthians 12:31 KJV)

PROMISE FROM GOD

"And whatsoever ye do, do it heartily, as to the Lord, and not unto men;"

"Knowing that of the Lord ye shall receive the reward of the inheritance: for ye serve the Lord Christ."

Work hard and happily at whatever you do, just as you were working for the Lord rather then people. Remember that the Lord will give you a legacy (inheritance) as your reward, and as the Master you are serving is Christ.

(Colossians 3:23, 24 KJV)

101. The first excuse in the Bible.

"And the man said, The woman whom thou gavest to be with me, she gave me of the tree, and I did eat.

It was Adam who came up with the first excuse. He accused (blamed) Eve, and in a roundabout way reprimanded (blamed) God for giving him "the woman." Then Eve accused (blamed) the serpent. Both attempted to excuse their action by accusing someone else.

(Genesis 3:12 KJV)

102. Other people who had poor excuses.

"And Sa'-rai said unto Abram, My wrong be upon thee: I have given my maid into thy bosom; and when she saw that she had conceived, I was despised in her eyes: the LORD judge between me and thee."

Sarai (Sarah) couldn't have children, so she gave her slave to Abram so as to have a child through her. Later Sarah reconsidered (had second thoughts) and blamed Abram for the entire thing.

(Genesis 16:5 KJV)

"And I said unto them, Whosoever hath any gold, let them break it off. So they gave it me: then I cast it into the fire, and there cam out this calf."

Aaron's faltering reason (lame excuse) for making an idol - something explicitly condemned by God - was that it simply occurred! How frequently we do something very similar, accusing our wrongdoing for conditions outside our ability to control. Be that as it may, the Bible plainly says we are totally responsible (accountable) for every one of our activities (Romans 14:12; Revelation 20:12).

(Exodus 32:24 KJV)

“And Saul said, They have brought them from the Am’-a-lek-ites: for the people spared the best of the sheep and of the oxen, to sacrifice unto the LORD thy God; and the rest we have utterly destroyed.”

Saul tried to justify his sinful actions with one excuse after another. Finally he ran out of excuses and lost his kingdom (I Samuel 15:26).

(I Samuel 15:15 KJV)

“And Peter said, Man, I know not what thou sayest. And immediately, while he yet spake, the cock crew.”

Peter had an excuse for not knowing Jesus-he wanted to save his life, or, best case scenario evade the mocking of being related with him. Ironically, it is the point at which we begin rationalizing about not knowing Jesus that we are in the most serious peril (most dangerous position).

(Luke 22:60 KJV)

103. Can we excuse ourselves from God’s work because we lack abilities or resources?

“And Moses said unto the LORD, O my Lord, I am not eloquent, neither heretofore, nor since thou hast spoken unto thy servant: but I am slow of speech, and of a slow tongue."

"And he said unto him, Oh my Lord, wherewith shall I save Israel? Behold, my family is poor in Ma-nas'-seh, and I am the least in my father's house."

"And the LORD said unto him, Surely I will be with thee, and thou shalt smite the Mid'-i-an-ites as one man."

Both Moses and Gideon thought they had a good excuse to escape serving God. Be that as it may, the capabilities God searches for are not quite the same as what we would anticipate. He frequently picks the most improbable individuals to accomplish his work so as to all the more successfully show his power. If you know God has called you to accomplish something stop trying to excuse yourself. He will give you the help and the strength you need to get the job done.

(Exodus 4:10; Judges 6:15, 16 KJV)

104. Can anyone be excused for not accepting the Lord?

"That at the name of Jesus every knee should bow, of things in heaven, and things in earth, and things under the earth;"

"And that every tongue should confess that Jesus Christ is Lord, to the glory of God the Father."

We as a whole have excuses for not putting God first - we're excessively occupied, we don't know how to witness, we'll do it later, we don't have the foggiest idea where to begin. Do you figure those excuses will hold up when we see God up close and personal (face-to-face)?

(Philippians 2:10, 11 KJV)

"For the invisible things of him from the creation of the world are clearly seen, being understood by the things that are made, even his eternal power and Godhead; so that they are without excuse:"

"I had a horrible father (or mother) and he (she) turned me against God." Another excuse that sounds good from the start. "I never heard." The Bible was too difficult to even consider understanding." "My folks never took me to church." All good excuses. Be that as it may, on Judgment Day, the Lord won't acknowledge (won't accept) them. Everybody has in any event had the declaration of nature, God's work. That by itself witnesses to his presence and power.

(Romans 1:20 KJV)

PROMISE FROM GOD

"And if ye call on the Father, who without respect of persons judgeth according to every man's work, pas the time of your sojourning here in fear:"

And remember that the heavenly Father to whom you pray has no top picks (no favorites) when he judges. He will pass judgment or reward you as per what you do. So you should live in reverent fear of him during your time as foreigners here on earth.

(I Peter 1:17 KJV)

FAILURE

105. What are some ways to prevent failure?

"And David said to Solomon his son, Be strong and of good courage, and do it: fear not, nor be dismayed: for the LORD God, even my God, will be with thee; he will not fail thee, nor forsake thee, until thou hast finished all the work for the service of the house of the LORD."

Courage and perseverance help prevent failure, especially if we know that God approves of the task we are doing.

(I Chronicles 28:20 KJV)

"Without counsel purposes are disappointed: but in the multitude of counsellors they are established."

Good advice helps prevent failure. A concert of wise counsel makes good music for success.

(Proverbs 15:22 KJV)

"They are new every morning: great is thy faithfulness."

God's great faithfulness resembles a crisp loaf of bread conveyed day by day to sustain us. It forestalls failure (helps prevent failure), however encourages us to start over again after we have failed.

(Lamentations 3:23 KJV)

106. How do I move ahead after I have failed?

"Moreover, brethren, I would not that ye should be ignorant, how that all our fathers were under the cloud, and all passed through the sea;"

"And were all baptized unto Moses in the cloud and in the sea;"

'And did all eat the same spiritual meat;"

"And did all drink the same spiritual drink: for they drank of that spiritual Rock that followed them: and that Rock was Christ."

"But with many of them God was not well pleased: for they were overthrown in the wilderness."

"Now these things were our examples, to the intent we should not lust after evil things, as they also lusted."

"Neither be ye idolaters, as were some of them; as it is written, THE PEOPLE SAT DOWN TO EAT AND DRINK, AND ROSE UP TO PLAY."

"Neither let us commit fornication, as some of them committed, and fell in one day three and twenty thousand."

"Neither let us tempt Christ, as some of them also tempted, and were destroyed of serpents."

"Neither murmur ye, as some of them also murmured, and were destroyed of the destroyer."

"Now all things happened unto them for ensamples: and they are written for our admonition, upon whom the ends of the world are come."

"Wherefore let him that thinketh he standeth take heed lest he fall."

These events happened as a warning to us! So that we would not crave evil things asn they did or worship idols as of them did. We are to remember that failure can be helpful to us. Failure can show us significant lessons about what to avoid a strategic distance from later on (what to avoid in the future). We need not repeat our mix-ups (mistakes)!

(I Corinthians 10:1-12 KJV)

"And the LORD said unto Joshua, Fear not, neither be thou dismayed; take all the people of war with thee, and arise, go up to A'-i: see, I have given into thy hand the king of A'-i, and his people, and his city, and his land:"

Try not to fear failing once more. Failure wins when you accept destruction and surrender (accepting defeat and giving up).

(Joshua 8:1 KJV)

"If we suffer, we shall also reign with him: if we deny him, he also will deny us:"

Failure isn't the end - it's about beginnings. You can recuperate and proceed onward.

There is an exit plan (There is always a way out).

(II Timothy 2:12 KJV)

"For we have not an high priest which cannot be touched with the feeling of our infirmities; but was in all points tempted like as we are, yet without sin."

"Let us therefore come boldly unto the throne of grace, that we may obtain mercy, and find grace to help in time of need."

We should understand that God's work isn't restricted nor limited by our failures. God doesn't dismiss or reject us in our shortcoming (weaknesses) but rather embraces us with the goal that we can receive strength to be all he intended us to be.

(Hebrews 4:15, 16 KJV)

PROMISE FROM GOD

"And he said unto me, My grace is sufficient for thee: for my strength is made perfect in weakness. Most gladly therefore will I rather glory in my infirmities, that the power of Christ may rest upon me."

Jesus Christ said unto us, My gracious favor is all you need. My power works best in your weakness. So now I am glad to boast about my weakness, so that the power of Christ may work through me.

(II Corinthians 12:9 KJV)

FAITH

107. Why I should have faith in God?

"And it shall be said in that day, Lo, this is our God; we have waited for him, and he will save us: this is the LORD; we have waited for him, we will be glad and rejoice in his salvation."

(Isaiah 25:9 KJV)

"Verily, verily, I say unto you, He that heareth my word, and believeth on him that sent me, hath everlasting life, and shall not come into condemnation; but is passed form death unto life."

Faith is the only way to get to heaven. It is the doorway to eternity. If God created eternity, then only through God would can we get there.

(John 5:24 KJV)

"Now faith is the substance of things hoped for, the evidence of things not seen."

(Hebrews 11:1 KJV)

108. How does faith in God affect my relationship with God? How does it change the way I live?

"And he believed in the LORD; and he counted it to him for righteousness."

(Genesis 15:6 KJV)

"Being justified freely by his grace through the redemption that is in Christ Jesus:"

"Whom God hath set forth to be a propitiation through faith in his blood, to declare his righteousness for the remission of sins that are past, through the forbearance of God;"

Sin breaks our relationship with God since it is disobedience, rebellion against God. A holy God can't live with unholy people. In any case, when we accept Jesus as Savior and ask that he forgive our sins, this simple act of faith makes us righteous in God's sight.

(Romans 3:24, 25 KJV)

"Thou wilt keep him in perfect peace, whose mind is stayed on thee: because he trusteth in thee."

Faith in God brings true peace of mind and heart since we know that we belong to him, and we know that one day all torment (pain) and suffering will end.

(Isaiah 26:3 KJV)

"For they that are after the flesh do mind the things of the flesh; but they that are after the Spirit the things of the Spirit."

(Romans 8:5 KJV)

"Now concerning spiritual gifts brethren, I would not have you ignorant."

(I Corinthians 12:1 KJV)

"But the fruit of the Spirit is love, joy, peace, longsuffering, gentleness, goodness, faith,"

"Meekness, temperance: against such there is no law."

Faith is welcoming God's Holy Spirit to live within us. It isn't only an act of the psyche (mind), but it taps us into the very resources of God with the goal that we have the ability to live in a completely new way. If God himself is living within us, our lives ought to be dramatically changed.

(Galatians 5:22, 23 KJV)

109. If I am struggling in my Christian life and have doubts, does it mean I have less faith?

"SIMON Peter, a servant and an apostle of Jesus Christ, to them that have obtained like precious faith with us through the righteousness of God and our Saviour Jesus Christ:"

"Grace and peace be multiplied unto you through the knowledge of God, and of Jesus our Lord,"

"According as his divine power hath given unto us all things that pertain unto life and godliness, through the knowledge of him that hath called us to glory and virtue:"

"Whereby are given unto us exceeding great and precious promises: that by these ye might be partakers of the divine nature, having escaped the corruption that is in the world through lust."

"And beside this, giving all diligence, add to your faith virtue; and to virtue knowledge;"

"And to knowledge temperance; and to temperance patience; and to patience godliness;"

"And to godliness brotherly kindness; and to brotherly kindness charity."

"For if these things be in you, and abound, they make you that ye shall neither be barren nor unfruitful in the knowledge of our Lord Jesus Christ."

"But he that lacketh these things is blind, and cannot see afar off, and hath forgotten that he was purged from his old sins."

...He has given all of us of his rich and superb promises...So bend over backwards to apply the advantages of these vows to your life...

(II Peter 1:1-9 KJV)

"And he said, Lord GOD, whereby shall I know that I shall inherit it?"

(Genesis 15:8 KJV)

"Now when John had heard in the prison the works of Christ, he sent two of his disciples,"

"And said unto him, Art thou he that should come, or do we look for another?"

Many people in the Bible whom we consider to be "pillars of faith" had snapshots (moments) of uncertainty. The key is to never abandon our faith and to consistently inquire as to whether, after some time, our lives have been drawing closer to or further away from God. In any event, during snapshots (moments) of uncertainty, you should invest the effort and discipline to allow your faith to grow.

(Matthew 11:2, 3 KJV)

PROMISE FROM GOD

"And they said, Believe on the Lord Jesus Christ, and thou shalt be saved, and thy house."

(Acts 16:31 KJV)

FAITHFULNESS

110. How do I cultivate faithfulness?

“Moreover they reckoned not with the men, into whose hand they delivered the money to be bestowed on workmen: for they dealt faithfully.”

(II Kings 12:15 KJV)

“Then the presidents and princes sought to find occasion against Daniel concerning the kingdom; but they could find none occasion nor fault; forasmuch as he was faithful, neither was there any error or fault found in him.”

Cultivate faithfulness by being honest and trustworthy.

(Daniel 6:4 KJV)

“”The LORD shall establish thee an holy people unto himself, as he hath sworn unto thee, if thou shalt keep the commandments of the LORD thy God, and walk in his ways.”

Cultivate faithfulness by obeying God’s Word.

(Deuteronomy 28:9 KJV)

"Let the deacons be the husbands of one wife, ruling their children and their own houses well."

Cultivate faithfulness by keeping your promises and commitments.

(I Timothy 3:12 KJV)

111. Why should I be faithful? Society tells me I should be able to do what I want.

"So shalt thou find favour and good understanding in the sight of God and man."

Faithfulness brings a good reputation and trust from other people.

(Proverbs 3:3, 4 KJV)

"And all the people that were in the gate, and the elders, said, We are witnesses. The LORD make the woman that is come into thine house like Ra'-chel and like Leah, which two did build the house of Israel: and do thou worthily in Eph'-ra-tah, and be famous in Beth'-le-hem:"

God chooses to accomplish great deeds through faithful people.

(Ruth 4:11 KJV)

"For we are made partakers of Christ, if we hold the beginning of our confidence stedfast unto the end;"

Faithfulness brings eternal rewards

(Hebrews 3:14 KJV)

112. Is God Faithful?

"And the heavens shall praise thy wonders, O LORD: thy faithfulness also in the congregation of the saints."

(Psalm 89:5 KJV)

"Know therefore that the LORD thy God, he is God, the faithful God, which keepeth covenant and mercy with them that love him and keep his commandments to a thousand generations;"

(Deuteronomy 7:9 KJV)

"But the Lord is faithful, who shall stablish you, and keep you from evil."

God is completely faithful. His faithfulness is so great it makes the angels sing!

(II Thessalonians 3:3 KJV)

"If we believe not, yet he abideth faithful: he cannot deny himself."

When others are unfaithful to us, we remain faithful. Otherwise, we become as faithless as they are.

(II Timothy 2:13 KJV)

PROMISE FROM GOD

"Being confident of this very thing, that he which hath begun a good work in you will perform it until the day of Jesus Christ:"

I am certain that God, who started the great work inside you, will proceed with his work until it is at last completed on that day when Jesus Christ returns once more.

(Philippians 1:6 KJV)

FAMILY

113. What is family? How does the Bible define "family?"

"Therefore shall a man leave his father and mother, and shall cleave unto his wife, and they shall be one flesh."

This express why a man leaves his father and mother and is joined to his wife, and the two are united into one.

(Genesis 2:24 KJV)

"Now therefore ye are no more strangers and foreigners, but fellow citizens with the saints, and of the household of God."

Christians are members of God's family.

(Ephesians 2:19 KJV)

"Of his own will begat he us with the word of truth, that w should be a kind of firstfruits of his creatures."

In God's goodness he chose to make us his own children.

The Bible talks about a natural (earthly) family made up of a couple and normally children, and the family of God, which is all believers united together by the bond of faith.

(James 1:18 KJV)

"So all Israel were reckoned by genealogies; and, behold, they were written in the book of the kings of Israel and Judah, who were carried away to Babylon for their transgression."

The Bible records several genealogies, all recorded by family units, demonstrating the family as focal and crucial to the development of people and of nations.

(I Chronicles 9:1 KJV)

"My son, keep thy father's commandment, and forsake not the law of thy mother:"

"Bind them continually upon thine heart, and tie them about thy neck."

"When thou goest, it shall lead thee; when thou sleepest, it shall keep thee; and when thou awakest, it shall talk with thee."

"For the commandment is a lamp; and the law is light; and reproofs of instruction are the way of life:"

Truth can be more effectively taught nowhere and modeled than in the family.

(Proverbs 6:20-23 KJV)

"And if it seem evil unto you to serve the LORD, choose you this day whom ye will serve; whether the gods which your fathers served that were on the other side of the flood, or the gods of the Am'-or-ites, in whose land ye dwell: but as for me and my house, we will serve the LORD."

The family is one of the greatest resources for imparting truth and affecting change in any community. This change is straightforwardly related to the family's spiritual commitment and zeal.

(Joshua 24:15 KJV)

"Lo, children are an heritage of the LORD: and the fruit of the womb is his reward."

The reward is the wonderful blessing of Children.

(Psalm 127:3 KJV)

114. Your responsibility to your family?

"And thou shalt teach them diligently unto thy children, and shalt talk of them when thou sittest in thine house, and when thou walkest by the way, and when thou liest down, and when thou risest up."

(Deuteronomy 6:7 KJV)

"Train up a child in the way he should go; and when he is old, he will not depart from it."

Teach your children the right path and when they are old, they shall stay on the right path.

To give them spiritual training and explain the gospel of Jesus Christ to them.

(Proverbs 22:6 KJV)

"When I call to remembrance the unfeigned faith that is in thee, which dwelt first in thy grandmother Lo'-is, and thy mother Eu-ni'-ce; and I am persuaded that in thee also."

I know that you earnestly trust the Lord, for you have the faith of your mother, Eunice, and your grandmother Lois.

(II Timothy 1:5 KJV)

"And that thou mayest tell in the ears of thy son, and of thy son's son, what things I have wrought in Egypt, and my signs which I have done among them; that ye may know how that I am the LORD."

You will be able to tell the great (wonderful) stories to your children and grandchildren about the wonderful things I am doing...To share spiritual experiences with them and help them to remember their spiritual heritage

(Exodus 10:2 KJV)

"That they may teach the young women to be sober, to love their husbands, to love their children,"

"To be discreet, chaste, keepers at home, good, obedient to their own husbands, that the word of God be not blasphemed."

(Titus 2:4, 5 KJV)

"CHILDREN, obey your parents in the Lord: for this is right."

"HONOUR THY FATHER AND MOTHER; which is the first commandment with promise."

"THAT IT MAY BE WELL WITH THEE, AND THOU MAYEST LIVE LONG ON THE EARTH."

"And, ye fathers, provoke not your children to wrath; but bring them up in the nurture and admonition of the Lord."

To love them and discipline them when necessary. To show them proper conduct. To be a decent good example (good role model).

(Ephesians 6:1-4 KJV)

"She looketh well to the ways of her household, and eateth not the bread of idleness."

She is alert to all that goes on in her household and does not have to bear the consequences of laziness.

(Proverbs 31:27 KJV)

"For I have told him that I will judge his house for ever for the iniquity which he knoweth; because his sons made themselves vile, and he restrained them not."

I have cautioned him ceaselessly that judgment is seeking his family, since his children are blaspheming God and he hasn't disciplined them.

(I Samuel 3:13 KJV)

"And his father had not displeased him at any time in saying, Why hast thou done so? and he also was a very goodly man; and his mother bare him after Ab'-sa-lom."

Now his father...had never disciplined him at any time, even by asking, "What are you doing?...

(I Kings 1:6 KJV)

"The rod and reproof give wisdom; but a child left to himself bringeth his mother to shame."

To train and censure a child produces astuteness (wisdom), but a mother is disrespected, shamed by a wayward child.

Neglect to show your children spiritual truths and ignoring discipline have disastrous outcomes.

(Proverbs 29:15 KJV)

115. Should I treat other believers like members of my own family?

"Finally, be ye all of one mind, having compassion one of another, love as brethren, be pitiful, be courteous:"

At long last, every one of you ought to be of one mind, brimming with compassion for each other, loving each other with delicate hearts and humble personalities.

God's family ought to have the entirety of the characteristics of family life, but reached out all through the family of God. We should love each other, feel for each other, and help each other. We ought to be bonded into a special family relationship.

(I Peter 3:8 KJV)

PROMISE FROM GOD

"The children of thy servants shall continue, and their seed shall be established before thee."

The children of your people will live in security. Their children's children will flourish in your presence.

(Psalm 102:28 KJV)

FEAR

116. What can I do when overcomed with fear? How do I find the strength to go on?

"GOD is our refuge and strength, a very present help in trouble."

"There will not we fear, though the earth be removed, and though the mountains be carried into the midst of the sea;"

God is our refuge and strength, constantly prepared to help in a tough situation (times of trouble). So we won't fear, regardless of whether seismic tremors come and the mountains disintegrate (crumble)` into the sea.

(Psalm 46:1, 2 KJV)

"Peace I leave with you, my peace I give unto you: not as the world giveth, give I unto you. Let not your heart be troubled, neither let it be afraid."

God vows to comfort us in our fear if we look for him when we are apprehensive (afraid). We have the certain confident assurance that he is with us in any condition.

(John 14:27 KJV)

117. When is fear good?

"Serve the LORD with fear and rejoice with trembling."

Since God is so great and compelling (mighty), and in light of the fact that he holds the power of life and death, we should have a sound, respectful (healthy), reverential fear of him. A healthy fear causes us keep our viewpoint about where we should be in our relationship with God.

(Psalm 2:11 KJV)

"Having therefore these promises, dearly beloved, let us cleanse ourselves from all filthiness of the flesh and spirit, perfecting holiness in the fear of God."

We should work toward complete purity because we fear God.

Healthy fear of God motivates us to strive for holiness.

(II Corinthians 7:1 KJV)

"And Moses called unto Joshua, and said unto him in the sight of all Israel, Be strong and of good courage: for thou must go with this people unto the land which the LORD hath sworn unto their fathers to give them; and thou shalt cause them to inherit it."

"And the LORD, he it is that doth go before thee; he will be with thee, he will not fail thee, neither forsake thee: fear not, neither be dismayed."

Fear can be acceptable in the event that it shows us courage. Joshua couldn't have genuinely gotten courage if he hadn't experienced fear. Fear gave him fearless character and instructed him to depend on and trust in God.

(Deuteronomy 31:7, 8 KJV)

118. When fear is not good.

“It is a fearful thing to fall into the hands of the living God.”

Fear is terrifying if we have to fall into he hands of the living God without having made peace with him.”

(Hebrews 10:31 KJV)

“And the men of the place asked him of his wife; and he said, She is my sister; for he feared to say, She is my wife; lest, said he, the men of the place should kill me for Rebekah; because she was fair to look upon.”

He was afraid to admit she was his wife.

(Genesis 26:7 KJV)

“And the children of Joseph said, The hill is not enough for us: and all the Ca’-naan-ites that dwell in the land of the valley have chariots of iron, both they who are of Beth-she’-an and her towns, and they who are of the valley of Jez’-re-el.”

"And Joshua spake unto the house of Joseph, even to E'-phra-im and to Ma-nas'-seh, saying, Thou art a great people, and hast great power: thou shalt not have one lot only:"

"But the mountain shall be thine; for it is a wood, and thou shalt cut it down: and the outgoings of it shall be thine: for thou shalt drive out the Ca'-naan-ites, though they have iron chariots, and though they be strong."

Fear is not good when it keeps us from doing the things we ought to do.

We are not meant to live in fear.

(Joshua 17:16-18 KJV)

PROMISES FROM GOD

"Fear thou not; for I am with thee: be not dismayed; for I am thy God: I will strengthen thee; yea, I will help thee; yea, I will uphold thee with the right hand of my righteousness."

(Isaiah 41:10 KJV)

FORGIVENESS

119. Can any sin be forgiven? There must be some sin too great to be forgiven.

"And it shall come to pass, that whosoever shall call on the name of the LORD shall be delivered: for in mount Zion and in Jerusalem shall be deliverance, as the LORD hath said, and in the remnant whom the LORD shall call."

Anyone who calls upon the name of the Lord shall be saved.

(Joel 2:32 KJV)

"Verily I say unto you, All sins shall be forgiven unto the sons of men, and blasphemies wherewith soever they shall blaspheme:"

"But he that shall blaspheme against the Holy Ghost hath never forgiveness, but is in danger of eternal damnation:"

(Mark 3:28, 29 KJV)

"For I am persuaded, that neither death, nor life, nor angels, nor principalities, nor powers, nor things present, nor things to come,"

"Nor height, nor depth, nor any other creature, shall be able to separate us from the love of God, which is in Christ Jesus our Lord."

Forgiveness does depend on the magnitude of the sin, however the magnitude of the forgiver's love. No sin is unreasonably great for God's finished and genuine love. The Bible does really make reference to one inexcusable sin-a disposition or an attitude of disobedient antagonistic vibe toward God that keeps us from tolerating his forgiving. The people who don't want his forgiveness are out of it's scope (out of it's reach).

(Romans 8:38, 39 KJV)

120. What does it really means to be forgiven?

"And you, that were sometime alienated and enemies in your mind by wicked works, yet now hath he reconciled"

"In the body of his flesh through death, to present you holy and unblameable and unreproveable in his sight:"

"If ye continue in the faith grounded and settled, and be not moved away from the hope of the gospel, which ye have heard, and which was preached to every creature which is under heaven; whereof I Paul am made a minister;"

You are holy and blameless as you stand before him without a single fault..

(Colossians 1:21-23 KJV)

"Come now, and let us reason together, saith the LORD: though your sins be as scarlet, they shall be as white as snow; though they be red like crimson, they shall be as wool."

No matter how deep the stain of your sins, I can remove it. I can make you as clean as freshly fallen snow.

(Isaiah 1:18 KJV)

"Repent therefore of this thy wickedness; and pray God, if perhaps the thought of thine heart may be forgiven thee."

"For I perceive that thou art in the gall of bitterness, and in the bond of iniquity."

Forgiveness frees us from slavery to sin.

(Acts 8:22, 23 KJV)

"But I say unto you, Love your enemies, bless them that curse you, do good to them that hate you, and pray for them which despitefully use you, and persecute you;"

Love your enemies and Pray for those who persecute you!

(Matthew 5:44 KJV)

"Saying, BLESSED ARE THEY WHO'S INIQUITIES ARE FORGIVEN, AND WHOSE SINS ARE COVERED."

Forgiveness brings great joy.

(Romans 4:7 KJV)

121. What can I do to activate God's loving forgiveness?

"If my people, which are called by my name, shall humble themselves, and pray, and seek my face, and turn from their wicked ways; then will I hear from heaven, and will forgive their sin, and will heal their land."

(II Chronicles 7:14 KJV)

"If we confess our sins, he is faithful and just to forgive us our sins, and to cleanse us from all unrighteousness."

(I John 1:9 KJV KJV)

"Return, ye backsliding children, and I will heal your backslidings. Behold, we come unto thee; for thou art the LORD our God."

"My wayward children, says the Lord, "come back to me, and I will heal your wayward hearts."

(Jeremiah 3:22 KJV)

PROMISE FROM GOD

"I, even I, am he that blotteth out thy transgressions for mine own sake, and will not remember thy sins."

I-yes, I alone-am the one who blots out your sins for my own sake and will never think of them again.

(Isaiah 43:25 KJV)

FRIENDSHIP

122. What is the true mark of friendship?

"A friend loveth at all times, and a brother is born for adversity."

Loyal always is a true friend, and a brother is born to help in time of need.

(Proverbs 17:17 KJV)

"AND it came to pass, when he had Saul, that the soul of Jonathan was knit with the soul of David, and Jonathan loved him as his own soul."

"And Saul took him that day, and would let him go no more home to his father's house."

"Then Jonathan and David made a covenant, because he loved him as his own soul."

"And Jonathan stripped himself of the robe that was upon him, and gave it to David, and his garments, even to his sword, and to his bow, and to his girdle."

Jonathan made a special vow to be David's friend.

Some friendships are temporary and some are enduring. Genuine friendships are stuck together with obligations of devotion (loyalty) and responsibility (commitment). They stay unblemished, remain intact, regardless of changing outer conditions.

(I Samuel 18:1-4 KJV)

123. What gets in the way of friendships?

"And David went out whithersoever Saul sent him, and behaved himself wisely; and Saul set him over the men of war, and he was accepted in the sight of all the people, and also in the sight of Saul's servants."

"And it came to pass as they came, when David returned from the slaughter of the Phi-lis'-tine, that the women came out of all cities of Israel, singing and dancing, to meet king Saul, with tabrets, with joy, and with instruments of musick."

"And the women answered one another as they played, and said, Saul hath slain his thousands, and David his ten thousands."

"And Saul was very wroth, and the saying displeased him; and he said, They have ascribed unto David ten thousands: and what can he have more but the kingdom?"

"And Saul eyed David from that day and forward."

"And it came to pass on the morrow, that the evil spirit of God came upon Saul, and he prophesied in the midst of the house: and David play with his hand, as at other times: and there was a javelin in Saul's hand."

"And Saul cast the javelin; for he said, I will smite David even to the wall with it. And David avoided out of his presence twice."

"And Saul was afraid of David, because the LORD was with him, and was departed from Saul."

"Therefore Saul removed him from him, and made him his captain over a thousand; and he went out and came in before the people."

"And David behaved himself wisely in all his ways; and the LORD was with him."

Jealously is the incredible dividing power of fellowships. Envy over what a friend has will before long go to outrage and harshness, making you separate yourself from the one you genuinely thought and cared about.

(I Samuel 18:5-13 KJV)

“Yea, mine own familiar friend, in whom I trusted, which did eat of my bread, hath lifted up his heel against me.”

My best friend, the one I trusted completely...has turned against me.

At the point when respect or worshiped is seriously harmed (damaged), even the dearest companion is in danger (at risk).

(Psalm 41:9 KJV)

“And when she had brought them unto him to eat, he took hold of her, and said unto her, Come lie with me, my sister.”

Many times friendships are destroyed when boundaries are violated.

(II Samuel 13:11 KJV)

“”And Joseph returned into Egypt, he, and his brethren, and all that went up with him to bury his father, after he had buried his father.”

“And when Joseph’s brethren saw that their father was dead, they said, Joseph will peradventure hate us, and will certainly requite us all the evil which we did unto him."

"And they sent a messenger unto Joseph, saying, They father did command before he died, saying,"

"So shall ye say unto Joseph, Forgive, I pray thee now, the trespass of thy brethren, and their sin; for they did unto thee evil; and now, we pray thee, forgive the trespass of the servants of the God of thy father. And Joseph wept when they spake unto him."

"And his brethren also went and fell down before his face; and they said, Behold, we be thy servants."

"And Joseph said unto them, Fear not: for am I in the place of God?"

"But as for you, ye thought evil against me; but God meant it unto good, to bring to pass, as it is this day, to save much people alive."

"Now therefore fear ye not: I will nourish you, and your little ones. And he comforted them, and spake kindly unto them."

These verses in Genesis tell us that Forgiveness restores broken relationships.

(Genesis 50:14-21 KJV)

124. What do I do when I'm having trouble making friends?

"All my inward friends abhorred me: and they whom I loved are turned against me."

(Job 19:19 KJV)

"The impotent man answered him, Sir, I have no man, when the water is troubled, to put me into the pool: but while I am coming, another steppeth down before me."

There are times when we all go through when it seems as though our friends have deserted us.

(John 5:7 KJV)

"Henceforth I call you not servants; for the servant knoweth not what his lord doeth: but I have called you friends; for all things that I have heard of my Father I have made known unto you."

(John 15:15 KJV)

"Let your conversation be without covetousness; and be content with such things as ye have: for he hath said, I WILL NEVER LEAVE THEE, NOR FORSAKE THEE."

We must remember first among all things that God is our constant friend and he will never leave nor forsake us.

(Hebrews 13:5 KJV)

"And be ye kind one to another, tenderhearted, forgiving one another, even as God for Christ's sake hath forgiven you."

Acts of kindness and generosity attract others to you.

(Ephesians 4:32 KJV)

125. Whether casual or romantic, male/female friendships involve unique pressures and temptations.

Does the Bible offer any guidelines for dating relationships?

"Charity suffereth long, and is kind; charity envieth not; charity vaunteth not itself, is not puffed up,"

“Doth not behave itself unseemly, seeketh not her own, is not easily provoked, thinketh no evil;”

“Rejoiceth not in iniquity, but rejoiceth in the truth;”

“Beareth all things, believeth all things, hopeth all things, endureth all things.”

Charity (Love) is patient, kind, is not jealous...Love does not demand its own way.

Paul’s timeless portrayal of Christian love turns into the standard of respect and decency that should stamp every one of our relationships, including our dating relationships.

(I Corinthians 13:4-7 KJV)

“But fornication, and all uncleanness, or covetousness, let it not be once named among you, as becoming saints;”

“Neither filthiness, nor foolish talking, nor jesting, which are not convenient: but rather giving of thanks.”

“For this ye know, that no whoremonger, nor unclean person, nor covetous man, who is an idolater, hath any inheritance in the kingdom of Christ and of God.”

"Let no man deceive you with vain words: for because of these things cometh the wrath of God upon the children of disobedience."

"Be not ye therefore partakers with them."

"For ye were sometimes darkness, but now are ye light in the Lord: walk as children of light:"

"(For the fruit of the Spirit is in all goodness and righteousness and truth;)"

"Proving what is acceptable unto the Lord."

"And have no fellowship with the unfruitful works of darkness, but rather reprove them."

"For it is a shame even to speak of those things which are done of them in secret."

"But all things that are reproved are made manifest by the light: for whatsoever doth make manifest is light."

"Whereforth he saith, Awake thou that sleepest, and arise from the dead, and Christshall give thee light."

"See then that ye walk curcumspectly, not as fools, but as wise,"

"Redeeming the time, because the days are evil."

"Wherefore be ye not unwise, but understanding what the will of the Lord is."

"And be not drunk with wine, wherein is excess; but be filled with the Spirit;"

Let there be no sexual immorality, impurity, or greed among you. Let the Holy Spirit fill and control you.

(Ephesians 5:3-5; 8-18 KJV)

"Ye have heard that it was said by them of old time, THOU SHALT NOT COMMIT ADULTERY:"

"But I say unto you, That whosoever looketh on a woman to lust after her hath committed adultery with her already in his heart."

"And if thy right eye offend thee, pick it out, and cast it from thee: for it is profitable for thee that one of thy members should perish, and not that thy whole body should be cast into hell."

"And if thy right hand offend thee, cut it off, and cast it from thee for it is profitable for thee that one of thy members should perish, and not that thy whole body should be cast into hell."

In sensational complexity to much that we find in our cutting edge world, Jesus calls us to a standard of sexual immaculateness in thought as well as in deed.

(Matthew 5:27-30 KJV)

PROMISE FROM GOD

"For where two or three are gathered together in my name, there am I in the midst of them."

For where two or three gather together because they are mine, I am there among them.

(Matthew 18:20 KJV)

FRUSTRATION

126. Why do we get frustrated?

"Thou shalt sow, but thou shalt not reap; thou shalt tread the olives, but thou shalt not anoint thee with oil; and sweet wine, but shalt not drink wine."

We somethings get frustrated when we work hard for something but it doesn't happen (it does not produce anything).

(Micah 6:15 KJV)

"Ye ask, and receive not, because ye ask amiss, that ye may consume it upon your lusts."

Here and there we are frustrated in our prayers, expecting certain answers that never come since we have an inappropriate thought processes (wrong motives). We neglect to perceive how God is protecting us from what will hurt us.

(James 4:3 KJV)

"And these things hast thou hid in thine heart: I know that this is with thee."

"If I sin, then thou markest me, and thou wilt not acquit me from mine iniquity."

"If I be wicked, woe unto me; and if I be righteous, yet will I not lift up my head. I am full of confusion; therefore see thou mine affliction;"

"For it increaseth. Thou huntest me as a fierce lion: and again thou shewest thyself marvellous upon me."

"Thou renewest thy witnesses against me, and increasest thine indignation upon me; changes and war are against me."

"Wherefore then hast thou brought me forth out of the womb? Oh that I had given up the ghost, and no eye had seen me!"

"I should have been as though I had not been; I should have been carried from the womb to the grave."

"Are not my days few? Cease then, and let me alone, that I may take comfort a little."

"Before I go whence I shall not return, even to the land of darkness and the shadow of death;"

"A land of darkness, as darkness itself; and of the shadow of death, without any order, and where the light is as darkness."

Pain and suffering bring frustration.

(Job 10:13-22 KJV)

"LORD, how long shall the wicked, how long shall wicked triumph?"

We should be frustrated by the evil around us.

(Psalm 94:3 KJV)

127. How am I respond to frustration?

"Every way of a man is right in his own eyes: but the LORD pondereth the hearts."

Man may think he is right in his own eyes, but God examines the hearts.

Looking at the wellspring or source of our frustration encourages us realize how to manage it. There is a major contrast between being frustrated in our mission to do good and being frustrated because we are not getting our way. Each must be managed in an unexpected way (each must be dealt with differently).

(Proverbs 21:2 KJV)

"And Moses cried unto the LORD, saying, What shall I do unto this people? they be almost ready to stone me."

(Exodus 17:4 KJV)

"When Jesus then lifted up his eyes, and saw a great company come unto him, he saith unto Philip, Whence shall we buy bread, that these may eat?"

"And this he said to prove him: for he himself knew what he would do."

We must recognize that some of our problems don't have a human solution. We must take them to God. Only he is able to handle some of our problems.

(John 6:5-7 KJV)

"And, ye fathers, provoke not your children to wrath: but bring them up in the nurture and admonition of the Lord."

We must be careful what we say when we are frustrated.

(Ephesians 6:4 KJV)

128. Does God ever cause frustration?

"He disappointeth the devices of the crafty, so that their hands cannot perform their enterprise."

God can frustrate the plans of the evil people.

(Job 5:12 KJV)

PROMISE FROM GOD

"Have not I commanded thee? Be strong and of good courage; be not afraid, neither be thou dismayed: for the LORD thy God is with thee whithersoever thou goest."

(Joshua 1:9 KJV)

GIVING

129. Why should we give?

"Bring ye all the tithes into the storehouse, that there may be meant in mine house, and prove me now herewith, saith the LORD of hosts, if I will not open you the windows of heaven, and pour you out a blessing, that there shall not be room enough to receive it."

We should give because God commands it. While we ought to never give just to receive something consequently (for that damages giving as an act of worship and love), God promises abundant blessings for the individuals who obey this command.

(Malachi 3:10 KJV)

"For God so loved the world, that he gave his only begotten Son, that whosoever believeth in him should not perish, but have everlasting life."

(John 3:16 KJV)

"And he looked up, and saw the rich men casting their gifts into the treasury."

"And he saw also a certain poor widow casting in thither two mites."

"And he said, Of a truth I say unto you, that this poor widow hath cast in more than they all:"

"For all these have of their abundance cast in unto the offerings of God: but she of her penury hath cast in all the living that she had."

The model for all giving is the heart of God. He loved such a lot of that he gave, not only belongings or cash, but his only Son to redeem a lost world.

(Luke 21:1-4 KJV)

"Thou shalt not delay to offer the first of thy ripe fruits, and of thy liquors: the firstborn of thy sons shalt thou give unto me."

"The first of the firstfruits of thy land thou shalt bring into the house of the LORD thy God. Thou shalt not seeth a kid in his mother's milk."

We should give a tithe because it demonstrates that God is first in our lives.

(Exodus 22:29; 23:19 KJV)

"Then the chief of the fathers and princes of the tribes of Israel, and the captains of thousands and of hundreds, with the rulers of the king's work, offered willingly."

"And gave for the service of the house of God of gold five thousand talents and ten thousand drams, and of silver ten thousand talents, and of brass eighteen thousands talents, and one hundred thousand talents of iron."

"And they with whom precious stones were found gave them to the treasure of the house of the LORD, by the hand of Je-hi'-el the Ger'-shon-ite."

Then the people rejoiced, for that they offered willingly, because with perfect heart they offered willingly to the LORD: and David the king also rejoiced with great joy."

"Wherefore David bless the LORD before all the congregation: and David said, Blessed be thou, LORD God of Israel our father, for ever and ever."

"Thine, O LORD, is the greatness, and the power, and the glory, and the victory, and the majesty: for all that is in heaven and in the earth is thine; thine is the kingdom, O LORD, and thou art exalted as head above all."

"Both riches and honour come of thee, and thou reignest over all; and in thine hand is power and might; and in thine hand it is to make great, and to give strength unto all."

"Now therefore, our God, we thank thee, and praise thy glorious name."

"But who am I, and what is my people, that should be able to offer so willingly after this sort? for all things come of thee, and of thine own have we given thee."

We should give since it advises us that the things we have are not what is most important.

(I Chronicles 29:6-14 KJV)

"I will freely sacrifice unto thee: I will praise thy name, O LORD; for it is good."

I will give a voluntary offering to you: O LORD, I will praise your name, O LORD; for it is good.

We should give out of a grateful heart.

(Psalm 54:6 KJV)

"Now he that ministereth seed to the sower both minister bread for your food, and multiply your seed sown, and increase the fruits of your righteousness;"

"Being enriched in every thing to all bountifulness, which causeth through us thanksgiving to God."

We should give to others so that God will be glorified.

(II Corinthians 9:10, 11 KJV)

"As every man hath receiveth the gift, even so minister the same one to another, as good stewards of the manifold grace of God."

The more we give of ourselves, the more God's generosity flows through us.

(I Peter 4:10 KJV)

130. How much should I give?

"Thou shalt truly tithe all the increase of thy seed, that the field bringeth forth year by year."

"And thou shalt eat before the LORD thy God, in the place which he shall choose to place his name there, the tithe of thy corn, of thy wine, and of thine oil, and the firstlings of thy herds and of thy flocks; that thou mayest learn to fear the LORD thy God always."

(Deuteronomy 14:22, 23 KJV)

"Honour the LORD with thy substance, and with the firstfruits of all thine increase:"

"So shall thy barns be filled with plenty, and thy presses shall burst out with new wine."

We should honor the Lord with the best part of everything your land produces. Then he will fill your barns with grain...

(Proverbs 3:9, 10 KJV)

"Upon the first day of the week let every one of you lay by him in store, as God hath prospered him, that there be no gatherings when I come.

On every Lord's Day, each of you should put aside some amount of money.

(I Corinthians 16:2 KJV)

"Every man according as he purposeth in his heart, so let him give; not grudgingly, or of necessity: for God loveth a cheerful giver."

We don't give reluctantly or in response to pressure, but cheerfully, gladly.

God wants you to give what you have, not what you don't have.

(II Corinthians 9:7 KJV)

"For if there be first a willing mind, it is accepted according to that a man hath, and not according to that he hath not."

While the Old Testament explicitly discusses giving one-tenth of what we make to God, the New Testament urges us to give out of an appreciative (grateful) heart. For some, this will mean giving unquestionably more than one-tenth!

(II Corinthians 8:12 KJV)

131. But I am just barely making it with my budget. How can I afford to tithe?

"And God is able to make all grace abound toward you; that ye, always having all sufficiency in all things, may abound to every good work:"

"(As it is written, HE HATH DISPERSED ABROAD; HE HATH GIVEN TO THE POOR: HIS RIGHTEOUSNESS REMAINETH FOR EVER."

In the event that we are not cautious, we will never think we have enough. The mystery of happiness is learning how to be content with what we have, regardless of whether it is a lot or little, and learning how to live abundantly even with little (see Philippians 4:11, 12).

(II Corinthians 9:8, 9 KJV)

PROMISE FROM GOD

"Give, and it shall be given unto you; good measure, pressed down, and shaken together, and running over, shall men give into your bosom. For with the same measure that ye mete withal it shall be measured to you again."

If you give, you will receive. Your blessing will come back to you in full measure, pushed down, shaken together to account for more, and running over. At all measure you use in giving - enormous or little - it will be used to measure what is given back to you.

(Luke 6:38 KJV)

GOODNESS

132. How should we "be good"?

"THERE was a man in the land of Uz, whose name was Job; and that man was perfect and upright, and one that feared God, and eschewed evil."

Job followed an arrangement for seeking after goodness that is straightforward in structure but so difficult in practice. When we avoid evil and honor God, we can't help but "be good."

(Job 1:1 KJV)

"And David said to Saul, Wherefore hearest thou men's words, saying, Behold, David seeketh thy hurt?"

"Behold, this day thine eyes have seen how that the LORD had delivered thee to day into mine hand in the cave: and some bade me kill thee: but mine eye spared thee; and I said I will not put forth mine hand against my lord; for he is the LORD'S anointed."

Returning good for evil is real victory.

(I Samuel 24:9, 10 KJV)

"Well reported of for good works; if she have lodged strangers, if she have washed the saints' feet, if she have relieved the afflicted, if she have diligently followed every good work."

Kind deeds are marks of goodness, which bring the respect of others.

(I Timothy 5:10 KJV)

"Behold, I have longed after thy precepts; quicken me in thy righteousness."

I long to obey your commandments! Renew my life with your goodness.

The Word of God is a clear statement of what God wants us to do and knows is best for us. To live as per God's Word is to live as indicated by his will, and that is carrying on with a good (holy) life.

(Psalm 119:40 KJV)

133. How then shall I show my appreciation to God for his goodness?

"O give thanks unto the LORD; for he is good; for his mercy endureth for ever."

(I Chronicles 16:34 KJV)

"I will praise the LORD according to his righteousness: and will sing praise to the name of the LORD most high."

(Psalm 7:17 KJV)

PROMISE FROM GOD

"A good man out of the good treasure of the heart bringeth forth good things: and an evil man out of the evil treasure bringeth forth evil things."

A good person produces good words from a good heart, and an evil person produces evil words from an evil heart.

(Matthew 12:35 KJV)

GOSSIP

134. Why Gossip is so bad?

"Thou shalt not go up and down as a talebearer among thy people: neither shalt thou stand against the blood of thy neighbor: I am the LORD."

Gossip is especially forbidden by God.

(Leviticus 19:16 KJV)

"A talebearer revealeth secrets: but he that is a faithful spirit concealeth the matter."

Gossip make poor companions. Avoid them. Gossips and trustworthy individuals work at far edges of the human range. Trustworthy individuals build you up. Gossips are destruction masters, attempting to tear you down.

(Proverbs 11:13 KJV)

"Being filled with all unrighteousness, fornication, wickedness, covetousness, maliciousness; full of envy, murder, debate, deceit, malignity; whisperers,"

God places gossip with greed, hate, envy, and murder.

(Romans 1:29 KJV)

"And withal they learn to be idle, wandering about from house to house; and not only idle, but tattlers also and busybodies, speaking things which they ought not."

Gossip often grows out of laziness.

We don't have anything preferable to do over lounging around talking about others. At that point we end up making statements we may later regret.

(I Timothy 5:13 KJV)

"Judge not, that ye be not judged."

Gossips places us in the spot of making a decision about (judging) others. In an official courtroom gossipy tidbits and suppositions are not permitted on the grounds that they may unreasonably influence the assessment of the jury. So it is when we transform our living rooms into courts where we sit as pass judgment and permit gossip and assessment to shading and frequently harm the reputation of other people who get no opportunity to defend themselves.

(Matthew 7:1 KJV)

"The words of a talebearer are as wounds, and they go down into the innermost parts of the belly."

Gossip hurts others. It also destroys your credibility if gossip proves false.

(Proverbs 18:8 KJV)

135. How do I stop gossip?

"Where no wood is, there the fire goeth out: so where there is no talebearer, the strife ceaseth."

Stop the chain of gossip with you! At the point when you hear gossip you can take care of business. You can choose not to spread it any further. Prevent the flames of gossip from spreading beyond you.

(Proverbs 26:20 KJV)

"If thou shalt hear say in one of thy cities, which the LORD thy God hath given thee to dwell there, saying,"

"Certain men, the children of Be'-li-al, are gone out from among you, and have withdrawn the inhabitants of their city, saying, Let us go and serve other gods, which ye have not known;"

"Then shalt thou enquire, and make search, and ask diligently; and, behold if it be truth, and the thing certain, that such abomination is wrought among you;"

You should look at the facts cautiously.

In the event that you don't know something is gossip, you should look cautiously into the issue without accepting what you have been told is true. Go to the source and get the facts straight.

(Deuteronomy 13:12-14 KJV)

"Therefore all things whatsoever ye would that men should do to you, do ye even so to them: for this is the law and the prophets."

The Golden Rule can likewise be applied to our discourse "Talk about others the same way as you might want them to talk about you."

(Matthew 7:12 KJV)

"Let no corrupt communication proceed out of your mouth, but that which is good to the use of edifying, that it may minister grace unto the hearers."

If we focus on what is good and helpful, gossip will find no foothold in our hearts.

(Ephesians 4:29 KJV)

"But now ye also put off all these; anger, wrath, malice, blasphemy, filthy communication out of your mouth."

"Lie not one to another, seeing that ye have put off the old man with his deeds;"

"And have put on the new man, which renewed in knowledge after the image of him that created him:"

"Where there is neither Greek nor Jew, circumcision nor uncircumcision, Barbarian, Scyth'-i-an, bond nor free: but Christ is all, and in all."

"Put on therefore, as the elect of God, holy and beloved, bowels of mercies, kindness, humbleness of mind, meekness, longsuffering;"

"Forbearing one another, and forgiving one another, if any man have a quarrel against any: even as Christ forgave you, so also do ye."

"And above all these things put on charity, which is the bond of perfectness."

"And let the peace of God rule in your hearts, to the which also ye are called in one body; and be ye thankful."

"Let the word of Christ dwell in you richly in all wisdom; teaching and admonishing one another in psalms and hymns and spiritual songs, singing with grace in your hearts to the Lord."

"And whatsoever ye do in word or deed, do all in the name of the Lord Jesus, giving thanks to God and the Father by him."

If you think you may be about to gossip, ask yourself, "Does the person I'm talking to need to know this? Is it true, accurate, and helpful?"

(Colossians 3:8-17 KJV)

PROMISE FROM GOD

"FOR HE THAT WILL LOVE LIFE, AND SEE GOOD DAYS, LET HIM REFRAIN HIS TONGUE FROM EVIL, AND HIS LIPS THAT THEY SPEAK NO GUILE:"

"For the Scriptures say, "If you want a happy life and good days, keep your tongue from speaking evil, and keep your lips from telling lies."

(I Peter 3:10 KJV)

GRACE

136. Where does grace come from? How do we receive it?

“For the LORD God is a sun and shield; the LORD will give grace and glory; no good thing will be withhold from them that walk uprightly.”

Grace begins with God and is given unreservedly by God. His gracefulness to us is our example for extending grace and benevolence (mercy) to other people.

Grace can’t be earned. It is openly given. It is God’s unmerited favor.

(Psalm 84:11 KJV)

“For by grace are ye saved through faith; and that not of yourselves: it is the gift of God:”

“Not of works, lest any man should boast.”

God saved you with his special blessing when you believed!

“It is by God’s grace that he chose to offer us the blessing of salvation. There is nothing we can do to earn it. We essentially receive it with faith and in thanks.

(Ephesians 2:8, 9 KJV)

"And of his fulness have all we received, and grace for grace."

"For the law was given by Moses, but grace and truth came by Jesus Christ."

In Old Testament times, God gave a code of laws to tell his people the best way to live for him until Jesus and the Holy Spirit came. Adhering to these laws didn't win salvation, however essentially delineated what an actual life changed by the Holy Spirit would resemble.

With the coming to Jesus, we never again need to thoughtlessly keep these laws in light of the fact that, by God's grace, we have been changed within so we went to live pure lives for him.

(John 1:16, 17 KJV)

"Let us therefore come boldly unto the throne of grace, that we may obtain mercy, and find grace to help in time of need."

When we arrive at God's very throne through prayer, we must linger to receive his grace."

(Hebrews 4:16 KJV)

137. How should I respond to God's grace?

"Being confident of this very thing, that he which hath begun a good work in you will perform it until the day of Jesus Christ:"

(Philippians 1:6 KJV)

"For we know the grace of our Lord Jesus Christ, that, though be was rich, yet for your sakes he became poor, that ye through his poverty might be rich."

"Grace involves self-sacrifice, giving something up in order to give it away."

(II Corinthians 8:9 KJV)

"O my God, incline thine ear, and hear; open thine eyes, and behold our desolations, and the city which is called by thy name: for we do no present our supplications before thee for our righteousness, but for thy great mercies."

Recognizing and asking for God's grace takes humility, for we understand that we don't merit it-which is actually why we need it.

(Daniel 9:18 KJV)

PROMISE FROM GOD

"The Lord is merciful and gracious, slow to anger, and plenteous in mercy."

(Psalm 103:8 KJV)

GREED

138. What will greed do to us?

"The desire of the slothful killeth him; for his hands refuse to labour."

"He coveteth greedily all the day long; but the righteous giveth and spareth not."

(Proverbs 21:25, 26 KJV)

"Yea, they are greedy dogs which can never have enough, and they are shepherds that cannot understand: they all look to their own way, every one for his gain, from his quarter."

Greed makes us uninformed of others' needs and makes us consider (think of) only ourselves.

(Isaiah 56:11 KJV)

"Thou shalt not covet thy neighbor's house, thou shalt not covet thy neighbour's wife, nor his manservant, nor his maidservant, nor his ox, nor has ass, nor anything that is thy neighbour's."

Envy, or coveting, is a type of greed. Greed can overwhelm us, moving us to follow things we know we should not have.

(Exodus 20:17 KJV)

"But now I have written unto you not to keep company, if any man that is called a brother be a fornicator, or covetous, or an idolater, or a railer, or a drunkard, or an extortioner; with such an one no not to eat."

In this passage of scripture God ranks greed with some of the worst kinds of sin.

(I Corinthians 5:11 KJV)

"And Re-ho-bo'-am went to She'-chem: for to She'-chem were all Israel come to make him king."

“And it came to pass, when Jer-o-bo’-am the son of Ne’-bat, who was in Egypt, whither he had fled from the presence of Solomon the king, heard it, that Jer-o-bo’-am returned out of Egypt.”

“And they sent and called him. So Jer-o-bo’-am and all Israel came and spake to Re-ho-bo’-am, saying,”

“Thy father made our yoke grievous; now therefore ease thou somewhat the grievous servitude of thy father, and his heavy yoke that he put upon us, and we will serve thee.”

“And he said unto them, Com again unto me after three days. And the people departed.”

“And king Re-ho-bo’-am took counsel with the old men that had stood before Solomon his father while he yet lived, saying, What counsel give ye me to return answer to this people?”

“And they spake unto him, saying, If thou be kind to this people, and please them, and speak good words to them, they will be thy servants for ever.”

“But he forsook the counsel which the old men gave him, and took counsel with the young men that were brought up with him, that stood before him.”

"And he said unto them, What advice give ye that we may return answer to this people, which have spoken to me, saying, Ease somewhat the yoke that thy father did put upon us?"

"And the young men that were brought up with him spake unto him, saying, Thus shalt thou answer the people that spake unto thee, saying, Thy father made our yoke heavy, but make thou it somewhat lighter for us; thus shalt thou say unto them, My little finger shall be thicker than my father's lions."

"For whereas my father put a heavy yoke upon you, I will put more to your yoke: my father chastised you with whips, but I will chastise you with scorpions."

"So Jer-o-bo'-am and all the people came to Re-ho-bo'-am on the third day, as the king bade, saying, Come again to me on the third day."

"And the king answered them roughly; and king Re-ho-bo'-am forsook the counsel of the old men."

"And answered them after the advice of the young men, saying, My father made your yoke heavy, but I will add thereto: my father chastised you with whips, but I chastiseyou with scorpions."

"So the king hearkened not unto the people: for the cause was of God, that the LORD might perform his word, which he spake by the hand of A-hi'-jah the Shi'-lo-nite to Jer-o-bo'-am the son of Ne'-bat."

"And when all Israel saw that the king would not hearken unto them, the people answered the king, saying, What portion have we in David? and we have none inheritance in the son of Jesse: every man to your tents, O Israel, now, David, see to thine own house. So all Israel went to their tents."

"But as for the children of Israel that dwelt in the cities of Judah, Re-ho-bo'-am reigned over them."

"Then king Re-ho-bo'-am sent Ha'do'-ram that was over the tribute; and the children of Israel stoned him with stones, that he died. But king Re-ho-bo'-am made speed to get him up to his chariot, to flee to Jerusalem."

"And Israel rebelled against the house of David unto this day."

Motivated by greed, Rehoboam squeezed too hard and divided his kingdom. The individuals who demand having everything regularly end up with close to nothing (very little) or nothing at all.

(II Chronicles 10:1-19 KJV)

"There is that scattereth, and yet increaseth; and there is that withholdeth more than is meet, but it tendeth to poverty."

The more you accumulate, the greater your chance of losing it all (losing everything).

(Proverbs 11:24 KJV)

PROMISE FROM GOD

"Lay not up for yourselves treasure upon earth, where moth and rust doth corrupt, and where theives break through and steal:"

"But lay up for yourselves treasures in heaven, where neither moth nor rust doth corrupt, and where thieves do not break through nor steal:"

"For where your treasure is, there will your heart be also."

(Matthew 6:19-21 KJV)

GRIEF

139. How Do I get over my grief?

“AND Joseph fell upon his father’s face, and wept upon him, and kissed him.”

“And Joseph commanded his servants the physicians to embalm his father: and the physicians embalmed Israel.”

“And forty days were fulfilled for him; for so are fulfilled the days of those which are embalmed: and the Egyptians mourned for him threescore and ten days.”

“And when the days of his mourning were past, Joseph spake unto the house of Pharaoh, saying, If now I have found grace in your eyes, speak, I pray you, in the ears of Pharaoh, saying,”

“My father made me swear, saying, Lo, I die; in my grave which I have digged for me in the land of Canaan, there shalt thou bury me. Now therefore let me go up, I pray thee, and bury my father, and I will come again.”

“And Pharaoh said, Go up, and bury thy father, according as he made thee swear.”

"And Joseph went up to bury his father: and with him went up all the servants of Pharaoh, the elders of his house, and all the elders of the land of Egypt,"

"And all of the house of Joseph, and his brethren, and his father's house: only their little ones, and their flocks, and their herds, they left in the land of Go'-shen."

"And there went up with him both chariots and horsemen: and it was a very great company."

"And they came to the threshingfloor of A'-tad, which is beyond Jordan, and there they mourned with a great and very sore lamentation: and he made a mourning for his father seven days."

"And when the inhabitants of the land, the Ca'-naan-ites, saw the mourning in the floor of A'-tad, they said, This is a grievous mourning to the Egyptians: wherefore the name of it was called A'-bel-miz'-ra-im, which is beyond Jordan."

"And his sons carried him into the land of Canaan, and buried him in the cave of the field of Mach-pe'-lah, which Abraham bought with the field for a possession of a burying place of E'-phron the Hit'-tite, before Mam'-re."

Joseph threw himself on his father and wept over him...

(Genesis 50:1-13 KJV)

"And A-him'-a-az called, and said unto the king, All is well. And he fell down to the earth upon his face before the king, and said, Blessed be the LORD thy God, which hath delivered up the men that lifted up their hand against my lord the king."

"And the king said, Is the young man Ab'-sa-lom safe? And A-him'-a-az answered, When Jo'-ab sent the king's servant, and me thy servant, I saw a great tumult, but I knew not what it was."

"And the king said unto him, Turn aside, and stand here. And he turned aside, and stood still."

"And, behold, Cu'-shi came; and Cu'-shi said, Tidings, my lord the king: for the LORD hath avenged thee this day of all them that rose up against thee."

"And the king said unto Ch'-shi, is the young man Ab'-sa-lom safe? And Cu'-shi answered, The enemies of my lord the king, and all that rise against thee to do thee hurt, be as that young man is."

"And the king was much moved, and went up to the chamber over the gate, and wept: and as he went, thus he said, "O my son Ab'-sa-lom, my son, my son Ab'-sa-lom!

Would God I had died for thee, O Ab'-sa-lom, my son, my son!"

First of all, we should perceive that grief is vital and significant. We need the opportunity to lament. It is an important part of closure since it permits us to actually and honestly communicate the way in which we feel.

(II Samuel 18:28-33 KJV)

"And Sarah was an hundred and seven and twenty years old: these were the years of the life of Sarah."

"And Sarah died in Kir'-jath-ar'-ba; the same is He'-bron in the land of Canaan; and Abraham came to mourn for Sarah, and to weep for her."

"And Abraham stood up from before his dead, and spake unto the sons of Heth, saying,"

"I am a stranger and a sojourner with you: give me a possession of a buryingplace with you, that I may bury my dead out of my sight."

"And the children of Heth annswered Abraham, saying unto him,"

"Hear us, my lord: thou art a mighty prince among us: in the choice of our sepulchres bury thy dead; none of us shall withhold from thee his sepulchre, but that thou mayest bury thy dead."

"And Abraham stood up, and bowed himself to the people of the land, even to the children of Heth."

"And he communed with them, saying, If it be your mind that I should bury my dead out of my sight; hear me, and intreat for me to E'-phron the son of Zo'-har,"

"That he may give me the cave of Mach-pe'-lah, which he hath, which is in the end of his field; for as much money as it is worth he shall give it me for a possession of a buryingplace amongst you."

"And E'-phron dwelt among the children of Heth: and E'-phron the Hit'-tite answered Abraham in the audience of the children of Heth, even of all that went in at the gate of his city, saying,"

"Nay, my lord, hear me: the field give I thee, and the cave that is therein, I give it thee; in the presence of the sons of my people give I it thee: bury thy dead."

"And Abraham bowed down himself before the people of the land."

"And he spake unto E'-phron in the audience of the people of the land, saying, But if thou wilt give it, I pray thee, hear me: I will give thee money for the field; take it of me, and I will bury my dead there."

"And E'-phron answered Abraham, saying unto him,"

"My lord, hearken unto me: the land is worth four hundred shek'-els of silver; what is that betwixt me and thee? Bury therefore thy dead."

"And Abraham hearkened unto E'-phron; and Abraham weighede to E'-phron the silver, which he had named in the audience of the sons of Heth, four hundred shek'-els of silver, current money with the merchant."

"And the field of E'-phrons, which was in Mach-pe'-lah, which was before Mam'-re, the field, and the cave which was therein, and all the trees that were in the field, that were in all the borders round about, were made sure"

"Unto Abraham for a possession in the presence of the children of Heth, before all that went in at the gate of his city."

"And after this, Abraham buried Sarah his wife in the cave of the field of Mach-pe'-lah before Mam'-re; the same is He'-bron in the land of Canaan."

"And the field, and the cave that is therein, were made sure unto Abraham for a possession of a buryingplace by the sons of Heth."

Take an interest (get involved) during the time spent grief. Set aside some effort to by and by grieve, but additionally become engaged with the essential strides to carry closure to your loss. We lament (we grieve) because we have had a positive experience - what we lost was important to us. Engaging during the time spent grief is a way of honoring what was meaningful.

(Genesis 23:1-20 KJV)

"A time to weep, and a time to laugh; a time to mourn, and a time to dance;"

Grief has its own season, but then the time has come to proceed onward to another. God wants us to wipe our tears, proceed onward, and be redemptive to other lamenting (grieving) people.

(Ecclesiastes 3:4 KJV)

"As one whom his mother comforteth, so will I comfort you; and ye shall be comforted in Jerusalem."

(Isaiah 66:13 KJV)

"Blessed be God, even the Father of our Lord Jesus Christ, the Father of mercies, and the God of all comfort;"

"Who comforteth us in all our tribulation, that we may be able to comfort them which are in any trouble, by the comfort wherewith we ourselves are comforted of God."

"For as the sufferings of Christ abound in us, so our consolation also aboundeth by Christ."

"And whether we be afflicted, it is for your consolation and salvation, which is effectual in the enduring of the same sufferings which we also suffer: or whether we be comforted, it is for your consolation and salvation."

"And our hope of you is stedfast, knowing, that as ye are partakers of the sufferings, so shall ye be also of the consolation."

God knows we grieve, understands our distresses and sorrows, and comforts us. God doesn't vow to protect us from grief, but to help us through it.

(II Corinthians 1:3-7 KJV)

"And God shall wipe away all tears from their eyes; and there shall be no more death, neither sorrow, nor crying, neither shall there be any more pain: for the former things are passed away."

Take hope that there will be no more grief in heaven.

(Revelation 21:4 KJV)

140. In what ways do we grieve?

"And Na-o'-mi said unto her two daughters in law, Go, return each to her mother's house: the LORD deal kindly with you, as ye have dealt with the dead, and with me."

The LORD grant you that ye may find rest, each of you in the house of her husband.

Then she kissed them; and they lifted up their voice, and wept."

"And they said unto her, Surely we will return with thee unto thy people."

"And Na-o'-mi said, Turn again, my daughters: why will ye go with me? are there yet any more sons in my womb, that they may be your husbands?

"Turn again, my daughters, go your way; for I am too old to have an husband. If I should say, I have hope, if I should have an husband also to night, and should also bear sons;"

"Would ye tarry for them till they were grown? would ye stay for them from having husbands? nay, my daughters; for it grieveth me much for your sakes that the hand of the LORD is gone out against me."

(Ruth 1:8-13 KJV)

"Wherefore the king said unto me, Why is thy countenance sad, seeing thou art not sick? this is nothing else but sorrow of heart. Then I was very sore afraid,"

"And said unto the king, Let the king live for ever; why should not my countenance be sad, when the city, the place of my fathers' sepulchres, lieth waste, and the gates thereof are consumed with fire?"

We grieve when we see loved ones hurt or in great need.

(Nehemiah 2:2, 3 KJV)

"When Jesus therefore saw her weeping, and the Jews also weeping which came with her, he groaned in the spirit, and was trooubled,"

"And said, Where have ye laid him? They said unto him, Lord, come and see."

"Jesus wept."

"Then said the Jews, Behold how he loved him!"

"And some of them said, Could not his man, which opened the eyes of the blind, have caused that even this man should not have died?"

(John 11:33-37 KJV)

"Now there was at Jop'-pa a certain disciple named Tab'-i-tha, which by interpretation is called Dor'-cas: this woman was full of good works and almsdeeds which she did."

"And it came to pass in those days, that she was sick, and died: whom when they had washed, they laid her in an upper chamber."

"And forasmuch as Lyd'-da was nigh to Jop'-pa, and the disciples had heard that Peter was there, they sent unto him two men, desiring him that he would not delay to come to them."

"Then Peter arose and went with them. When he was come, they brought him into the upper chamber: and all the widows stood by him weeping, and shewing the coats and garments which Dor'-cas made, while she was with them."

"But Peter put them all forth, and kneeled down, and prayed; and turning him to the body said, Tab'-i-tha, arise. And she opened her eyes: and when she saw Peter, she sat up."

"And he gave her his hand, and lifted her up, and when he had called the saints and widows, presented her alive."

"And it was known throughout all Jop'-pa; and many believed in the Lord."

We grieve over the death of a loved one.

(Acts 9:36-42 KJV)

"Be afflicted, and mourn, and weep: let your laughter be turned to mourning, and your joy to heaviness."

May there be tears for an inappropriate (wrongful, sinful) things you have done. May there be grief and profound anguish. May there be trouble rather than chuckling, and agony rather than joy.

(James 4:9 KJV)

"For godly sorrow worketh repentance to salvation not to be repented of: but the sorrow of the world worketh death."

God can use sorrow in our lives to help us turn away from sin and seek salvation.

We ought to truly lament (grieve) for our transgressions (sins) and ask God to forgive them. Until Christ has cleansed us of those sins, we nurture them and they keep on hiding inside us. Confession and forgiveness will purge sin and wipe away the tears that unconfessed sin brings.

(II Corinthians 7:10 KJV)

"O Jerusalem, Jerusalem, which killest the prophets, and stonest them that are sent unto thee; how often would I have gathered thy children together, as a hen doth gather her brood under her wings, and ye would not!"

We should grieve over lost souls.

(Luke 13:34 KJV)

PROMISE FROM GOD

"He healeth the broken in heart, and bindeth up their wounds.

(Psalm 147:3)

GUILT

141. How are we guilty?

"For all have sinned, and come short of the glory of God;"

(Romans 3:23 KJV)

"Therefore to him that knoweth to do good, and doeth it not, to him it is sin."

Sin is not only doing wrong things, but not doing good (right) things.

(James 4:17 KJV)

"For whosoever shall keep the whole law, and yet offend in one point, he is guilty of all."

A person who keeps all the law and breaks one of the laws is as guilty as sure as a "little sin" as with a "big sin (sin is sin regardless of big or little or much or one).

(James 2:10 KJV)

142. How can I be freed from guilt?

"Who can understand his errors? cleanse thou me from secret faults."

"Keep back thy servant also from presumptuous sins; let them not have dominion over me: then shall I be upright, and I shall be innocent from the great transgression."

By avoiding from sin as much as could reasonably be expected and confessing any transgression (sin) to God. Blame or guilt is the result of bad behavior, wrongdoing (sin).

(Psalm 19:12, 13 KJV)

"And by him all that believe are justified from all things, from which ye could not be justified by the law of Moses."

Everybody who believes in him is liberated from all blame/guilt and proclaimed right with God.

This is a superb example of the grace of God. We should simply accept God's unconditional gift of salvation. This implies accepting that God sent his Son, Jesus, to die for our sins that we are no longer blameworthy (guilty) for them.

(Acts 13:39 KJV)

"Only acknowledge thine iniquity, that thou hast transgressed against the LORD thy God, and hast scattered thy ways to the strangers under every green tree, and ye have not obeyed my voice, saith the LORD.

There is a significant cost to recognizing guilt and admitting sin, but a much greater cost in the event that we don't.

(Jeremiah 3:13 KJV)

"If we confess our sins, he is faithful and just to forgive us our sins, and to cleanse us from all unrighteousness."

Prayer and confession free us from guilt. Try not to let blameworthy emotions (guilty emotions) over sin keep you from prayer, your only means for confessing to God and reestablishing (restoring) your relationship with him.

(I John 1:9 KJV)

PROMISE FROM GOD

"And by him all that believe are justified from all things, from which ye could not be justified by the law of Moses."

Everyone who believes in him is freed from all guilt and declared right with God...

(Acts 13:39 KJV)

HABITS

143. Some Bad habits the Bible talks about.

"He that committeth sin is of the devil; for the devil sinneth from the beginning. For this purpose the Son of God was manifested, that he might destroy the works of the devil."

When people continue to sin, they show they belong to the Devil.

Sin is a habit none of us can lick totally, but a pattern of sinful living shows that we may not be not serious about following God.

(I John 3:8 KJV)

"And Pharoh said, I will let you go, that ye may sacrifice to the LORD your God in the wilderness; only ye shall not go very far away: intreat for me."

"And Moses said, Behold, I go out from thee, and I will intreat the LORD that the swarms of flies may depart from Pharaoh, from his servants, and from his people, to morrow: but let not Pharaoh deal deceitfully any more in not letting the people go to sacrifice to the LORD."

"And Moses went out from Pharaoh, and intreated the LORD."

"And the LORD did according to the word of Moses; and he removed the swarms of flies from Pharaoh, from his servants, and from his people; there remained not one."

"And Pharaoh hardened his heart at this time also, neither would he let the people go."

Pharaoh built up a habit for lying and wanting his own way. Both of these are propensities we can without much of a stretch slip into, but they are terrible, even disastrous.

(Exodus 8:28-32 KJV)

"And when the people complained, LORD heard it; and his anger was kindled; and the fire of the LORD burnt among them, and consumed them that were in the uttermost parts of the camp."

The Israelites built up a habit for whining, complaining. Standard grumbling (complaining) can rapidly transform into harshness, bitterness.

(Numbers 11:1 KJV)

"And withal they learn to be idle, wandering about from house to house; and not only idle, but tattlers also and busybodies, speaking things which they ought not."

They are likely to become lazy and spend their time gossiping.

An excess of time and too little to even think about doing can be fruitful ground for negative behavior patterns. This inaction, idleness (laziness) makes it simple to build up the negative behavior pattern of gossip. Here Paul was discussing widows, who had additional time on their hands in light of the fact that the church took care of them.

Be that as it may, the rule concerns every one of us.

(I Timothy 5:13 KJV)

144. How do we deal with bad habits?

"For we know that the law is spiritual: but I am carnal, sold under sin."

"For that which I do I allow not: for what I would, that do I not; but what I hate, that do I."

"If then I do that which I would not, I consent unto the law that it is good."

"Now then it is no more I that do it, but sin that dwelleth in me."

"For I know that in me (that is, in my flesh,) dwelleth no good thing: for to will is present with me; but how to perform that which is good I find not."

"For the good that I would I do not: but the evil which I would not, that I do."

"Now if I do that I would not, it is no more I that do it, but sin that dwelleth in me."

"I find then a law, that, when I would do good, evil is present with me."

"For I delight in the law of God after the inward man:"

"But I see another law in my members, warring against the law of my mind, and bringing me into captivity to the law of son which is in my members."

"O wretched man that I am! who shall deliver me from the body of this death?"

"I thank God through Jesus Christ our Lord. So then with the mind I myself serve the law of God; but with the flesh the law of sin."

Have you at any point felt along these lines? Paul uncovers to us perhaps the most ideal approaches to manage negative behavior patterns (bad habits) see the truth about them and admit them genuinely. Paul realized that he was unable to kick the habit for transgression (sin) medium-term. However, he realized that, with God's assistance, he could gain ground each day. Similarly we may need to surrender a habit in stages, one day at a time.

(Romans 7:14-25 KJV)

"Love not the world, neither the things that are in the world. If any man love the world, the love of the Father is not in him."

Stop loving the evil world and all it presents or offers to you.

Sin frequently shows up flawless, lovely, attractive and appealing. Similarly, unfortunate habits regularly feel good despite the fact that we know they are eventually bad for us. Ending a negative behavior pattern (bad habit) can be hard, in light of the fact that we are losing something we like.

Comprehend that there might be a lamenting procedure. However, this pain over losing a bad habit brings the more profound bliss (deeper joy) that we are doing what is pleasing to God.

(I John 2:15 KJV)

"Set your affection on things above, not on things on the earth."

We should allow heaven fill our thoughts.

We must replace a bad habit with something good.

(Colossians 3:2 KJV)

145. How do we develop good habits?

"Not forsaking the assembling of ourselves together, as the manner of some is; but exhorting one another and so much the more, as ye see the day approaching."

Getting together as believers is a good habit because it furnishes fundamental fellowship with other believers, it builds up the habit for group Bible study, it keeps us occupied when we may somehow or another be slipping into negative behavior patterns (bad habits), and it offers an accountability group.

(Hebrews 10:25)

"Then Isaac sowed in that land, and received in the same year an hundredfold: and the LORD blessed him."

"And the man waxed great, and went forward, and grew until he became very great:"

"For he had possession of flocks, and possession of herds, and great store of servants: and the Phi-lis'-tines envied him."

"For all the wells which his father's servants had digged in the days of Abraham his father, the Phi-lis'-tines had stopped them, and filled them with earth."

"And A'bim'-e-lech said unto Isaac, Go from us; for thou art much mightier than we."

"And Isaac departed thence, and pitched his tent in the valley of Ge'-rar, and dwelt there."

"And Isaac digged again the wells of water, which they had digged in the days of Abraham his father; for the Phi-lis'-tines had stopped them after the death of Abraham: and he called their names after the names by which his father had called them."

"And Issac's servants digged in the valley, and found there a well of springing water."

"And the herdsmen of Ge'-rar did strive with Isaac's herdmen, saying, The water of our's: and he called the name of the well E'-sek; because they strove with him."

"And they digged another well, and strove for that also: and he called the name of it Sit'-nah."

"And he removed from thence, and digged another well; and for that they strove not: and he called the name of it Re-ho'-both; and he said, For now the LORD hath made room for us, and we shall be fruitful in the land."

"And he went up from thence to Be'-er-she'-ba."

"And the LORD appeared unto him the same night, and said, I am the God of Abraham thy father: fear not, for I am with thee, and will bless thee, and multiply thy seed for my servant Abraham's sake."

"And he builded an altar there, and called upon the name of the LORD, and pitched his tent there: and there Isaac's servants digged a well."

Isaac sought after a habit of peace. Right now, implied wandering ceaselessly from the wellspring of the conflict, the Philistines, even at extraordinary expense (great cost).

(Genesis 26:12-25 KJV)

"Blessed be the LORD, because he hath heard the voice of my supplications."

"The LORD is my strength and my shield; my heart trusted in him, and I am helped: therefore my heart greatly rejoiceth; and with my song will I praise him."

"The LORD is their strength, and he is the saving strength of his anointed."

As a youngster, David built up the habit for conversing with God, singing songs about him, and composing psalms. This helped him to trust in and follow God for his whole life.

(Psalm 28:6-8 KJV)

"Know ye not, that to whom ye yield yourselves servants to obey, his servants ye are to whom ye obey, whether of sin unto death, or of obedience unto righteousness?"

"But God be thanked, that ye were servants of sin, but ye have obeyed from the heart that form of doctrine which was delivered you."

Submission is a choice. We day by day stand at the intersection, choosing corrupt ways or God's way. The ways are not our own, but the choice is ours.

(Romans 6:16, 17 KJV)

PROMISE FROM GOD

"For they that are after the flesh do mind the things of the flesh; but they that are after the Spirit the things of the Spirit."

"For to be carnally minded is death; but to be spiritually minded is life and peace."

Those who are controlled by the evil nature consider wicked things, however those who are controlled by the Holy Spirit consider things that please the Spirit. In the event that your wicked nature controls your mind, there is death. Be that as it may, if the Holy Spirit controls your mind, there is life and peace.

(Romans 8:5, 6 KJV)

HAPPINESS

146. Where do we get real, lasting happiness?

"Looking unto Jesus the author and finisher of our faith; who for the joy that was set before him endured the cross, despising the shame, and is set down at the right hand of the throne of God."

Keep your eyes on Jesus!

(Hebrews 12:2 KJV)

"Praise ye the LORD. Blessed is the man that feareth the LORD, that delighteth greatly in his commandments."

Fear God and trust in him; delight in doing his commands.

(Psalm 112:1 KJV)

"I have set the LORD always before me: because he is at my right hand, I shall not be moved."

"Therefore my heart is glad, and my glory rejoiceth: my flesh also shall rest in hope."

Happiness depends on God's presence within us, which brings genuine or true contentment..

(Psalm 16:8, 9 KJV)

"But the fruit of the Spirit is love, joy, peace, longsuffering, gentleness, goodness, faith,"

"Meekness, temperance: against such there is no law."

The presence of the Holy Spirit in our lives produces joy.

(Galatians 5:22,23 KJV)

"Blessed are they that keep his testimonies, and that seek him with the whole heart."

Happy are the people who obey his commandments and search for him with all their hearts."

(Psalm 119:2 KJV)

"And having this confidence, I know that I shall abide and continue with you all for your furtherance and joy of faith."

"I will continue with you so that you will grow and experience the joy of your faith."

Faith in God brings happine4ss, for God has promised that when we4 truly seek him, we will surely find him (Jeremiah 29:13, 14)

(Philippians 1:25 KJV)

"His lord said unto him, Well done, thou good and faithful servant: thou hast been faithful over a few things, I will make thee ruler over many things; enter thou into the joy of thy lord."

One gains a deep sense of satisfaction when he does a job well done and is an occasion for joy."

(Matthew 25:21 KJV)

147. How can I be happy in the midst of difficult circumstances?

"For this thing I besought the Lord thrice, that it might depart from me."

"And he said unto me, My grace is sufficient for thee: for my strength is made perfect in weakness. Most gladly therefore will I rather glory in my infirmities, that the power of Christ may rest upon me."

"Therefore I take pleasure in infirmities, in reproaches, in distresses for Christ's sake: for when I am weak, then am I strong."

(II Corinthians 12:8-10 KJV)

"Beloved, think it not strange concerning the fiery trial which is to try you, as though some strange thing happened unto you:"

But rejoice, inasmuch as ye are partakers of Christ's sufferings; that, when his glory shall be revealed, ye may be glad also with exceeding joy."

Our difficult situations help us better understand what Christ went through for us and makes us partners with him.

(I Peter 4:12, 13 KJV)

"By whom also we have access by faith into this grace wherein we stand, and rejoice in hope of the glory of God."

We joyfully and confidentially look forward to sharing God's glory.

(Romans 5:2 KJV)

"For ye had compassion of me in my bonds, and took joyfully the spoiling of your goods, knowing in yourselves that ye have in heaven a better and an enduring substance."

Hope in God's promises of eternal life can make us happy, because we know what we are by and by experiencing (what we are going through) will one day end.

(Hebrews 10:34 KJV)

"And they departed from the presence of the council, rejoicing that they were counted worthy to suffer shame for his name."

(Acts 5:4 KJV 1)

"Rejoice in the Lord always: and again I say, Rejoice."

"I know both how to be abased, and I know how to abound; everywhere and in all things I am instructed both to be full and to be hungry, both to abound and to suffer need."

(Philippians 4:4, 12 KJV)

"My brethren, count it all joy when ye fall into divers temptations:"

Whenever trouble comes your way, let it be an opportunity for joy.

God doesn't promise brief happiness, in reality the Bible assumes problems will come our direction. Be that as it may, God promises lasting joy for each one of us who believe and trust in him. This kind of happiness (joy) stays with us despite our problems.

(James 1:2 KJV)

148. Is it possible to be happy when we have nothing material?

"Yet I will rejoice in the LORD, I will joy in the God of my salvation."

Habakkuk portrayed in the past verses an express depriving of material possessions. At that point this wonderful verse reasons that still he will find joy in the Lord.

(Habakkuk 3:18 KJV)

"There is that maketh himself rich, yet hath nothing: there is that maketh himself poor, yet hath great riches."

Material riches can bring spiritual poverty. Material poverty can bring spiritual riches. It is conceivable to have the both kinds of wealth, but keep an eye out on that you are tangibly "blessed, lest your blessing become a curse.

(Proverbs 13:7 KJV)

"Lay not up for yourselves treasures upon earth, where moth and rust doth corrupt, and where thieves break through and steal:"

But lay up for yourselves treasure in heaven, where neither moth nor rust doth corrupt, and where thieves do not break through nor steal:"

"But lay up for yourselves treasures in heaven, where neither moth nor rust doth corrupt, and where thieves do not break through nor steal:"

"For where your treasure is, there will your heart be also."

(Matthew 6:19-21 KJV)

PROMISE FROM GOD

"The desire of the righteous is only good: but the expectation of the wicked is wrath."

Those who are godly can look forward to happiness, while the wicked can expect only wrath.

(Proverbs 11:23 KJV)

HATRED

149. Is it ever appropriate to hate anyone or anything?

"Thou shalt not hate thy brother in thine heart: thou shalt in any wise rebuke thy neighbour, and not suffer sin upon him."

Not only are you not to hate your brother, but do not nurse hatred in your heart for any of your relatives.

(Leviticus 19:17 KJV)

"A time to love, and a time to hate; a time of war, and a time of peace."

(Ecclesiastes 3:8 KJV)

"Ye that love the LORD, hate evil: he preserveth the souls of his saints; he delivereth them out of the hand of the wicked."

Those who love the lord, hate evil.

(Psalm 97:10 KJV)

“Whosoever hateth his brother is a murderer: and ye know that no murderer hath eternal life abiding in him.”

He who hates another Christian is a murderer at heart.

(I John 3:15 KJV)

“Ye have heard that it hath been said, THOU SHALT LOVE THY NEIGHBOUR, and hate thine enemy.”

“But I say unto you, Love your enemies, bless them that curse you, do good to them that hate you, and pray for them which despitefully use you, and persecute you;”

(Matthew 5:43, 44 KJV)

150. What causes hatred?

“Now the works of the flesh are manifest, which are these; Adultery, fornication, uncleanness, lasciviousness.”

"Idolatry, witchcraft, hatred, variance, emulations, wrath, strife, seditions, heresies,"

"Envyings, murders, drunkenness, revellings, and such like: of the which I tell you before, as I have also told you in time past, that they which do such things shall not inherit the kingdom of God."

"But the fruit of the Spirit is love, joy, peace, longsuffering, gentleness, goodness, faith,"

"Meekness, temperance: against such there is no law."

Hatred originates from following our own wicked desires. Rather, we should allow the Holy Spirit to fill our lives, ruling out hatred.

(With the Holy Spirit working within our lives we have no room for hatred).

(Galatians 5:19-23 KJV)

"Then went Ha'-man forth that day joyful and with a glad heart; but when Ha'-man saw Mor'-de-cai in the king's gate, that he stood not up, nor moved for him, he was full of indignation against Mor'-de-cai."

Haman hated Mordecai in light of the fact that he wouldn't bow down before him. This unimportant jealousy, a desire for acknowledgment/recognition, made Haman to crazy contempt, insane that would not be fulfilled until Mordecai was executed (killed). Be cautious! Insignificant desire (petty desire) can prompt hatred, which can prompt vicious contemplations (violent thoughts) or actions.

(Esther 5:9 KJV)

151. How do we let go of hatred?

"a SOFT answer turneth away wrath: but grievous words stir up anger."

Get rid of anger. Anger leads to bitterness, which leads to hatred.

(Proverbs 15:1 KJV)

"He hath shewed thee, O man, what is good; and what doth the LORD require of thee, but to do justly, and to love mercy, and to walk humbly with thy God?"

Mercy and humility are powerful weapons against hatred.

(Micah 6:8 KJV)

"Let all bitterness, and wrath, and anger, and clamour, and evil speaking, be put away from you, with all malice:"

"And be ye kind one to another, tenderhearted, forgiving one another, even as God for Christ's sake hath forgiven you."

Forgiveness stops hatred.

(Ephesians 4:31, 32 KJV)

"Wives, submit yourselves unto your own husbands, as it is fit in the Lord."

"Husbands, love your wives, and be not bitter against them."

Humble "submission" and "love" cast out hatred.

(Colossians 3:18, 19 KJV)

"I have given them thy word; and the world hath hated them, because they are not of the world, even as I am not of the world."

The world hates Christians because they do not belong to the world.

(John 17:14 KJV)

"If ye be reproached for the name of Christ, happy are ye; for the spirit of glory and of God resteth upon you: on their part he is evil spoken of, but on your part he is glorified."

"But let none of you suffer a murderer, or as a thief, or as an evildoer, or as a busybody in other men's matters."

"Yet if any man suffer as a Christian, let him not be ashamed; but let him glorify God on this behalf."

"For the time is come that judgment must begin at the house of God: and if it first begin at us, what shall the end be of them that obey not the gospel of God?"

"And IF THE RIGHTEOUS SCARCELY BE SAVED, WHERE SHALL THE UNGODLY AND THE SINNER APPEAR?"

Wherefore let them that suffer according to the will of God commit the keeping of their souls to him in well doing, as unto a faithful Creator."

There is no shame to suffer for being a Christian…

Those who love sin hate the people who are against sin. If you stand firm against sin, anticipate, expect opposition.

(I Peter 4:14-19 KJV)

PROMISE FROM GOD

"If a man say, I love God, and hateth his brother, he is a liar; for he that loveth not his brother whom he hath seen, how can he love God whom he hath not seen?"

If someone says, "I love God," however hates another Christian, that individual is a liar; if we don't love individuals we can see, how might we love God, whom we have not seen?

(I John 4:20 KJV)

HEALING

152. From what do we need to be healed?

"For he had one only daughter, about twelve years of age, and she lay a dying. But as he went the people thronged him."

His only child was twelve years old, a little girl who was dying.

(Luke 8:42 KJV)

"And there came a leper to him, beseeching him, and kneeling down to him, and saying unto him, If thous wilt, thou canst make me clean."

We desire to be healed from sickness and disease.

(Mark 1:40 KJV)

"The Spirit of the Lord God is upon me; because the LORD hath anointed me to preach good tidings unto the meek; he hath sent me to bind up the brokenhearted, to proclaim liberty to the captives, and the opening of the prison to them that are bound;"

Our broken hearts need healing and restoration.

(Isaiah 61:1 KJV)

"Thou hast turned for me my mourning into dancing; thou hast put off my sackcloth, and grided me with gladness;"

We need healing from sorrow.

(Psalm 30:11 KJV)

“He hath put forth his hands against such as be at peace with him: he hath broken his covenant.”

As my friend he has betrayed me.

We need healing from the pain of betrayal.

(Psalm 55:20 KJV)

“For the wages of sin is death; but the gift of God is eternal life through Jesus Christ our Lord.”

(Romans 6:23 KJV)

“Who forgiveth all thine iniquities; who healeth all thy diseases;”

“Who redeemeth thy life from destruction; who crowneth thee with lovingkindness and tender mercies;”

He forgives all my sins.

We need to be heal from sin.

(Psalm 103:3, 4 KJV)

"A merry heart doeth good like a medicine: but a broken spirit drieth the bones."

A happy heart is acceptable medication, however a wrecked spirit saps a person's strength. There is a connection between a healthy spirit and an uplifting or positive attitude.

(Proverbs 17:22 KJV)

153. How does God heal?

"And Isaiah said, Take a lump of figs. And they took and laid it on the boil, and he recovered."

Make an ointment from figs and spread it over the boil. They did this, and Hezekiah recovered! Through physicians and medicine.

(II Kings 20:7 KJV)

"I will never forget thy precepts: for with them thou hast quickened me."

I will not forget thy commandments: for with them thy hast used them to restore my joy and health.

(Psalm 119:93 KJV)

"And when he had looked round about on them with anger, being grieved for the hardness of their hearts, he saith unto the man, Stretch forth thine hand. And he stretched it out; and his hand was restored whole as the other."

(Mark 3:5 KJV)

"And it came to pass, when he was in a certain city, behold a man full of leprosy; who seeing Jesus fell on his face, and besought him, saying, Lord, if thou wilt, thou canst make me clean."

"And he put forth his hand, and touched him, saying, I will: be thou clean. And immediately the leprosy departed from him."

There are times healing comes through miracles.

(Luke 5:12, 13 KJV)

"And again he entered into Ca-per'-na-um after some days; and it was noised that he was in the house."

"And straightway many were gathered together, insomuch that there was no room to receive them, no, not so much as about the door: and he preached the word unto them."

"And they come unto him, bringing one sick of palsy, which was borne of four."

"And when they could not come nigh unto him for the press, they uncovered the roof where he was: and when they had broken it up, they let down the bed wherein the sick of the palsy lay."

"When Jesus saw their faith, he said unto the sick of palsy, Son, thy sins be forgiven thee."

Healing can come through the faith of friends.

(Mark 2:1-5 KJV)

"Have mercy upon me, O LORD; for I am weak: O LORD, heal me; for my bones are vexed."

Heal me, LORD, for my body is in agony.

(Psalm 6:2 KJV)

"Is any among you afflicted? let him pray. Is any merry? Let him sing psalms."

"Is any sick anomg you? Let him call for the elders of the church; and let them pray over him, anointing him with oil in the name of the Lord."

"And the prayer of faith shall save the sick, and the Lord shall raise him up; and if he have committed sins, they shall be forgiven him."

"Confess your faults one to another, and pray for another, that ye may be healed.

The effectual fervent prayer of a righteous man availeth much."

They should call for the elders of the church and have them pray over them...

(James 5:13-16 KJV)

"O Lord, by these things men live, and in all these things is the life of my spirit: so wilt thou recover me, and make me to live."

The Lord's discipline is good, for it leads to life and health.

(Isaiah 38:16 KJV)

"And Esau hated Jacob because of the blessing wherewith his father blessed him: and Esau said in his heart, The days of mourning for my father are at hand; then will I slay my brother Jacob."

"And Esau ran to meet him, and embraced him, and fell on his neck, and kissed him: and they wept."

Esau hated Jacob… Then Esau ran to meet him and embraced him affectionately and kissed him. Both of them were in tears.

(Healing through time)

(Genesis 27:41; 33:4 KJV)

"But he was wounded for our transgressions, he was bruised for our iniquities: the chastisement of our peace was upon him; and with his stripes we are healed."

By death Christ brought us life. Through woundedness he brought us healing. by accepting our punishment, he set us free.

(Isaiah 53:5 KJV)

154. Why doesn't God always heal people?

"For this thing I besought the Lord thrice, that it might depart from me."

"And he said unto me, My grace is sufficient for thee: for my strength is made perfect in weakness. Most gladly therefore will I rather glory in my infirmities, that the power of Christ may rest upon me."

Jesus' power works best in your weakness.

God's power is amplified through our shortcomings and ailments, if we permit him to work within us.

(II Corinthians 12:8, 9 KJV)

155. How do I deal with it when I'm not healed?

"Therefore I take pleasure in infirmities, in reproaches, in necessities, in persecutions, in distresses for Christ's sake: for when I am weak, then am I strong."

We can anticipate having God's power work through us in an uncommon manner (special way). At the point when God works through the frail (the weak), clearly what happened needed to happen as a result of him, along these lines demonstrating to the world his love and power.

(II Corinthians 12:10 KJV)

PROMISE FROM GOD

"But unto you that fear my name shall the Sun of righteousness arise with healing in his wings; and ye shall go forth, and grow up as calves of the stall."

But for you who fear my name, the Sun of righteousness will arise with mending (healing) in his wings. Also, you will go free, jumping with joy like calves let out to pasture.

(Malachi 4:2 KJV)

HELP

156. Will God help us when we truly seek him?

"But when they in their trouble did turn unto the LORD God of Israel, and sought him, he was found of them."

Whenever you were in distress and turned to the Lord..and sought him out, you found him. In other words, prayer is the life saver (the life line) that connects us to the Lord

God our helper.

(II Chronicles 15:4 KJV)

"If any of you lack wisdom, let him ask of God, that giveth to all men liberally, and upbraideth not; and it shall be given him."

(If you want to know what God wants you to do, ask him, and he will gladly tell you).

(James 1:5 KJV)

"But my God shall supply all your need according to his riches in glory by Christ Jesus."

God has a full supply house and a full supply system. It's free for the asking, but we must ask.

(Philippians 4:19 KJV)

157. How can I help others?

"But whoso hath this world's good, and seeth his brother have need, and shutteth up his bowels of compassion from him, how dwelleth the love of God in him?

If one of you has cash enough to live well and sees a brother or sister in need and will not help (or refuse to help) - how to can God's love be in that person?

(I John 3:17 KJV)

"Learn to do well; seek judgment, relieve the oppressed, judge the fatherless, plead for the widow."

God expects us top offer our abundance with the individuals who have less. Poor people, orphans, and widows are symbolic of numerous who have less than we and need our help.

(Isaiah 1:17 KJV)

"Two are better than one; because they have a good reward for their labour."

"For if they fall, the one will lift up his fellow; but woe to him that is alone when he falleth; for he hath not another to help him up."

When we attempt to help ourselves, we are constrained by the very wellspring of our weaknesses. Be that as it may, when we rely upon one another for help, we may supplement (complement) each other's strengths and weaknesses.

(Ecclesiastes 4:9, 10 KJV)

"I COMMEND unto you Phe'-be our sister, which is a servant of the church which is at Cen'-chre-a:"

"That ye receive her in the Lord, as becometh saints, and that ye assist her in whatsoever business she hath need of you; for she hath been a succourer of many, and of myself also."

Help her in every way you can, for she has helped many in their needs.

Interdependence is healthy. We are made to live in community, which infers that we are to be continually helping one another. Requesting help is certifiably not a sign of weakness, however a characteristic of unity.

(Romans 16:1, 2 KJV)

"As every man hath receiveth the gift, even so minister the same one to another, as good stewards pf the manifold grace of God."

"Of any man speak, let him speak as the oracles of God; if any man minister, let him do it as of the ability which God giveth: that God in all things may be glorified through Jesus Christ, to whom be praise and dominion for ever and ever. A-men'."

We must be helpful to others, but for some it is a spiritual gift.

(I Peter 4:10, 11 KJV)

PROMISE FROM GOD

"Is any thing too hard for the LORD? At the time appointed I will return unto thee, according to time of life, and Sarah shall have a son."

The Emphasis is: Is Any Thing Too Hard For The LORD?

(Genesis 18:14 KJV)

HONESTY

158. Why is it so important to be honest?

"Who shall ascend into the hill of the LORD? or who shall stand in his holy place?"

"He that hath clean hands, and a pure heart; who hath not lifted up his soul unto vanity, nor sworn deceitfully."

"He shall receive the blessing from the LORD, and righteousness from the God of his salvation.

Who may climb the mountain of the LORD? Who may stand in his holy place: Only those whose hands and hearts are pure, who don't worship idols and never tell lies... to inherit God's goodness.

(Psalm 24:3-5 KJV)

"A just weight and balance are the LORD'S: all the weights of the bag are his work."

The Lord demands reasonableness (fairness) in each business deal; he sets the standard.

God expects it.

(Proverbs 16:11 KJV)

"Either make the tree good, and his fruit good; or else make the tree corrupt, and his fruit corrupt: for the tree is known by his fruit."

A tree is identified by its fruit.

(Matthew 12:33 KJV)

"He that is faithful in that which is least is faithful also in much: and he that is unjust in the least is unjust also in much."

If you cheat even a little, you won't be honest with greater responsibilities.

(Luke 16:10 KJV)

"Holding faith, and a good conscience; which some having put away concerning faith have made shipwreck;"

Always keep your conscience clear. For some people have purposely violated their consciences; as a result, their faith has been wrecked.

(I Timothy 1:19 KJV)

"Thou shalt not have in thy bag divers weights, a great and a small."

"Thou shalt not have in thine house divers measures, a great and a small."

"But thou shalt have a perfect and just weight, a perfect and just measure shalt thou have: that thy days may be lengthened in the land which the LORD thy God giveth thee."

"For all that do such things, and all that do unrighteously, are an abomination unto the LORD thy God."

God blesses us when we are concerned not about how much we get but about being honest in getting it.

(Deuteronomy 25:13-16 KJV)

"The integrity of the upright shall guide them: but the perverseness of transgressors shall destroy them."

Good people are guided by their honesty, treacherous people are destroyed by their dishonesty.

Dishonesty and deception are a type of subjugation since we are continually attempting to hide our genuine thought processes (hide our real motives). There is freedom in honesty because it takes into consideration forgiveness, vulnerability, positive change, and healing.

(Proverbs 11:3 KJV)

"For I say, through grace given unto me, to every man that is among you, not to think of himself more highly than he ought to think; but to think soberly, according as God hath dealt to every man the measure of faith."

Be honest in your estimate of yourselves.

Honestly evaluating our walk with the Lord is the only way to keep growing in faith.

(Romans 12:3 KJV)

159. Does honesty always mean telling everything I know?

"A time to rend, and a time to sew; a time to keep silence, and a time to speak;"

A time to be quiet and a time to speak up.

(Ecclesiastes 3:7 KJV)

"Seest thou a man that is hasty in his words? there is more hope of a fool than of him."

There is more hope for a fool than for someone who speaks without thinking.

(Proverbs 29:20 KJV)

"The words of a man's mouth are as deep waters, and the wellspring of wisdom as a flowing brook."

(Proverbs 18:4 KJV)

"Let your speech be always with grace, seasoned with salt, that ye may know how ye ought to answer every man."

Let your conversation be gracious and effective.

Honestly not be mistaken for gossip. Because you know something doesn't mean you need to inform everybody regarding it. Honesty (Trustworthiness) additionally includes integrity, uprightness, ensuring that what you state is helpful and builds others up as opposed to tearing them down. The person who thinks before speaking is often the wisest.

(Colossians 4:6 KJV)

PROMISE FROM GOD

"The lip of truth shall be established for ever; but a lying tongue is but for a moment."

Truth stands the test of time; lies are soon exposed.

(Proverbs 12:19 KJV)

HOPE

160. What can I do when things seem hopeless?

"NOW there was a certain man of Ra-math-a'-im-zo'-phim, of mount E'-phra-im, and his name was El'-kia-nah, the son of Jer'-o-ham, the son of E-li'-hu, the son of To'-hu, the son of Auph, an Eph'-rath-ite:"

"And he had two wives; the name of the one was Hannah, and the name of the other Pe-nin'-nah: and Pe-nin'-nah had children, but Hannah had no children."

"And this man went up out of his city yearly to worship and to sacrifice unto the LORD of hosts in Shi'-loh. And the two sons of E'-li, Hoph'-ni and Phin'-e-has, the priests of the LORD were there."

"And when the time was that El'-ka-nah offered, he gave to Pe-nin'-nah his wife, and to all her sons and her daughters, portions:"

"But unto Hannah he gave a worthy portion; for he loved Hannah: but the LORD had shut up her womb."

"And her adversary also provoked her sore, for to make her fret, because the LORD had shut up her womb."

"And as he did so year by year, when she went up to the house of the LORD, so she provoked her; therefore she wept, and did not eat."

"Then said El'-ka-nah her husband to her, Hannah, why weepest thou? and why eatest thou not? and why is thy heart grieved? am I not better to the than ten sons?"

"So Hannah rose up after they had eaten in Shi'-loh, and after they had drunk. Now E'-li the priest sat upon a seat by a post of the temple of the LORD."

"And she was in bitterness of soul, and prayed unto the LORD, and wept sore."

"And she vowed a vow, and said, O LORD of hosts, if thou wilt indeed look on the affliction of thine handmaid, and remember me, and not forget thine hand, but wilt give unto thine handmaid a man child, then I will give him unto the LORD all the days of his life, and there shall no razor come upon his head."

"And it came to pass, as she continued praying before the LORD, that E'-li marked her mouth."

"Now Hannah, she spake in her heart; only her lips moved, but her voice was not heard: therefore E'-li thought she had been drunken."

"And E'-li said unto her, How long wilt thou be drunken? put away thy wine from thee."

"And Hannah answered and said, No, my lord, I am a woman of a sorrowful spirit: I have drunk neither wine nor strong drink, but have poured out my soul before the LORD."

"Count not thine handmaid for a daughter of Be'-li-al: for out of the abundance of my complaint and grief have I spoken hitherto."

"Then E'-li answered and said, Go in peace: and the God of Israel grant thee thy petition that thou hast asked of him."

"And she said, Let thine handmaid find grace in thy sight. So the woman went her way, and did eat, and her countenance was no more sad."

"And they rose up in the morning early, and worshipped before the LORD, and returned, and came to their house to Ra'-mah: and El'-ka-nah remembered her."

"Wherefore it came to pass, when the time was come about after Hannah had conceived, that she bare a son, and called his name Samuel, saying, Because I have asked him of the LORD."

"And the man El'-ka-nah, and all his house, went up to offer unto the LORD the yearly sacrifice, and his vow."

But Hannah went not up; for she said unto her husband, I will not go up until the child be weaned, and then I will bring him, that he may appear before the LORD, and there abide for ever."

"And El'-ka-nah her husband said unto her, Do what seemeth thee good; tarry until thou have weaned him; only the LORD establish his word. So the woman abode, and gave her son suck until she weaned him."

"And when she had weaned him, she took him up with her, witrh three bullocks, and on e'-phah of flour, and a bottle of wine, and brought him unto the house of the LORD in Shi'-loh: and the child was young."

"And they slew a bullock, and brought the child to E'-li."

"And she said, Oh my lord, as thy soul liveth, my lord, I am the woman that stood by thee here, praying unto the LORD."

"For this child I prayed; and the LORD hath given me my petition which I asked of him:"

"Therefore also I have lent him to the LORD; as long as he liveth he shall be lent to the LORD. And he worshipped the Lord there."

Amidst Hannah's misery (hopelessness), she prayed to God, knowing that if any hope was to be discovered, it would be found in him (The Lord).

(I Samuel 1:1-28 KJV)

"And it came to pass, as we went to prayer, a certain damsel possessed with a spirit of divination met us, which brought her masters much gain by soothsaying:"

"The same followed Paul and us, and cried, saying, These men are the servants of the most high God, which shew unto us the way of salvation."

"And this did she many days. But Paul, being grieved, turned and said to the spirit, I command thee in the name of Jesus Christ to come out of her. And he came out the same hour."

"And when her masters saw that the hope of their gains was gone, they caught Paul and Silas, and drew them into the marketplace unto the rulers,"

"And brought them to the magistrates, saying, These men, being Jews, do exceedingly trouble our city."

"And teach customs, which are not lawful for us to receive, neither to observe, being Romans."

"And the multitude rose up together against them: and the magistrates rent off their clothes, and commanded to beat them."

"And when they had laid many stripes upon them, they cast them into prison, charging the jailor to keep them safely:"

"Who, having received such a charge, thrust them into the inner prison, and made their feet fast in the stocks."

"And at midnight Paul and Silas prayed, and sang praises unto God and the prisoners heard them."

"And suddenly there was a great earthquake, so that the foundations of the prison were shaken: and immediately all the doors were opened, and every one's bands were loosed."

"And the keeper of the prison awaking out of his sleep, and seeing the prison doors open, he drew out his sword, and would have killed himself, supposing that the prisoners had been fled."

"But Paul cried with a loud voice, saying, Do thyself no harm: for we are all here."

"Then he called for a light, and sprang in, and came trembling, and fell down before Paul and Silas,"

"And brought them out, and said, Sirs, what must I do to be saved?"

"And they said, Believe on the Lord Jesus Christ, and thou shalt be saved, and thy house."

"And they spake unto him the word of the Lord, and to all that were in his house."

"And he took them the same hour of the night, and washed their stripes; and was baptized, he and all his, straightway."

"And when he had brought them into his house, he set meal before them, and rejoiced, believing in God with all his house."

Paul and Silas were waiting for capital punishment for preaching about Jesus, yet right now in what appeared to be a hopeless situation, they sang praises to God. Why?

Because they had an eternal perspective.

(Acts 16:16-34 KJV)

"The hope of the righteous shall be gladness: but the expectation of the wicked shall perish."

The hopes of the godly result in happiness, but the expectations of the wicked are all in vain.

Regardless of how sad things appear to be here on earth, in Christ we have ultimate eternal hope. Those who don't know Jesus Christ have only their own misery (hopelessness) to stick to.

(Proverbs 10:28 KJV)

"Wait on the LORD: be of good courage, and he shall strengthen thine heart: wait, I say, on the LORD."

Hope is trusting God to act in his good timing.

(Psalm 27:14 KJV)

“Ye looked for much, and, lo, it came to little; and when ye brought it home, I did blow upon it. Why? Saith the LORD of hosts. Because of mine house that is waste, and ye run every man unto his own house.”

You hoped for rich harvests, but they were poor. And when you brought your harvest home, I blew it away. Why? Because my house lies in ruins, says the LORD ALMIGHTY, while you are all busy building your own fine houses.

When we honor God, our hopes can be richly fulfilled.

(Haggai 1:9 KJV)

161. How can I put my hope in God?

“For thou art my hope, O Lord God; thou art my trust from my youth.”

Who but God controls what’s to come (the future)? Who but God has a home for us that is everlasting? Who but God forgives our transgressions (sins)? Who but God can give us a life that lasts forever (Life Eternal)? No wonder he is our hope!

(Psalm 71:5 KJV)

"For we are saved by hope: but hope that is seen is not hope: for what a man seeth, why doth he yet hope for?"

Salvation comes through trust in Jesus Christ, believing he will do for us what he has promised. Hope is expecting that he will give us everlasting life and that we will live with him forever. We can't see these things, but we can hope with assurance, for our hope is built on a trust in the most trustworthy one of all, Jesus Christ.

(Romans 8:24 KJV)

"NOW faith is the substance of things hoped for, the evidence of things not seen."

We have faith in God to do what he has promised, and we can be certain beyond a shadow of a doubt that he will. So our hopes are not inactive expectations (idle hopes), but based on the solid foundation of his trustworthiness.

(Hebrews 11:1 KJV)

"For I know the thoughts that I think toward you, saith the LORD, thoughts of peace, and not of evil, to give you and expected end."

I know the plans I have for you, says the LORD. They are plans for good and not for disaster, to give you a future and a hope.

(Jeremiah 29:11 KJV)

"Brethren, I count not myself to have apprehended: but this one thing I do, forgetting those things which are behind, and reaching forth unto those things which are before."

"I press toward the mark for the prize of the high calling of God in Christ Jesus."

God never plans evil or hopelessness for his people. And his ultimate plan is to give us eternal life with him in heaven, where pain, sorrow, and suffering are gone forever.

(Philippians 3:13, 14 KJV)

PROMISE FROM GOD

"And thou shalt be secure, because there is hope; yea, thou shalt dig about thee, and thou shalt take thy rest in safety."

(Job 11:18 KJV)

HOSPITALITY

162. Does everyone need to practice hospitality, or is it a special gift for just a few?

"Distributing to the necessity of saints; given to hospitality."

Get in the habit of inviting guests home for dinner.

(Romans 12:13 KJV)

"Use hospitality one to another without grudging."

Cheerfully share your home with those who need a meal or a place to stay.

(I Peter 4:9 KJV)

"Beloved, thou doest faithfully whatsoever thou doest to the brethren, and to strangers:"

You are doing a good work for God when you faithfully take care of brethren and strangers who are passing through.

(3 John 1:5 KJV)

"Be not forgetful to entertain strangers: for thereby some have entertained angels unawares."

Do not forget to show hospitality to strangers, for some who have done this have entertained angels without knowing it.

(Hebrews 13:2 KJV)

"It is not to deal thy bread to the hungry, and that thou bring the poor that are cast out to thy house? when thou seest the naked, that thou cover him; and that thou hide not thyself from thine own flesh?"

I want you to impart your food to the hungry and to invite poor wanderers into your homes.

(Isaiah 58:7 KJV)

"For I was an hungred. And ye gave me meat: I was thirsty, and ye gave me drink: I was a stranger, and ye took me in:"

Naked, and ye clothed me: I was sick, and ye visited me: I was in prison, and ye came unto me."

I was hungry, and you fed me. I was thirsty, and you gave me a drink...I was sick, and your cared for me. I was in prison, and you came to me.

(Matthew 25:35, 36 KJV)

"Then said he also to him that bade him, When thou makest a dinner or a supper, call not thy friends, nor thy brethren, neither thy kinsmen, nor thy rich neighbours; lest they also bid thee again, and a recompence be made thee.'

"But when thou makest a feast, call the poor, the maimed, the lame, the blind:"

"And thou shalt be blessed; for they cannot recompense thee; for thou shalt be recompensed at the resurrection of the just."

While hospitality in additional measure is positively and certainly a gift, we are all called to practice hospitality as best we can, for it is a genuine demonstration of benevolence (a true act of kindness), and it encourages and strengthens others. It is likewise a statement of thankfulness (gratefulness) for what God has done for us.

(Luke 14:12-14 KJV)

163. What is the most important part of hospitality?

"But one thing is needful: and Mary hath chosen that good part, which shall not be taken away from her."

There is really only a single thing worth being concerned about. Mary has found it-and I won't remove it from her!

The most significant part of hospitality is simply the sharing of ourselves and our Lord with others. The Bible mentions both elaborate dinners (Gen. 18:1-8; II Samuel 3:20) and spontaneous get-togethers (Acts 10:23). Do not to be intimidated by hospitality, thinking you should plan huge dinners and clean the house. Simply share yourself and Christ with others.

(Luke 10:42 KJV)

164. Is hospitality more than the way we welcome others into our homes?

"The Lord give mercy unto the house of On-e-siph'-o-rus; for he oft refreshed me, and was not ashamed of my chain:"

May the Lord show special kindness to Onesiphorus and all his family because he often visited and encouraged me. He was never ashamed of me because I was in prison.

Hospitality reaches beyond our own homes to places of confinement such as hospitals, nursing homes, or prisons.

(II Timothy 1:16 KJV)

PROMISE FROM GOD

"Then shall the righteous answer him, saying, Lord, when saw we thee an hungred, and fed thee? or thirsty, and gave thee drink?"

"When saw we thee a stranger, and took thee in? or naked, and clothed thee?"

"Or when saw we thee sick, or in prison, and came unto thee?"

"And the King shall answer and say unto them, Verily I say unto you, inasmuch as ye have done it unto one of the least of these my brethren, ye have done it unto me."

Then the righteous ones will answer, "Lord, when did we observe you hungry and feed you. Or then again parched and give you something to drink? Or on the other hand an outsider and give you cordiality? Or on the other hand naked and give you dress? When did we ever observe you sick or in jail, and visit you?" And the King will let them know, "I promise you, when you did it to one of the least of these my brothers and sisters, you were doing it to me!"

(Matthew 25:37-40 KJV)

HUMILITY

165. How important is it to avoid pride and seek humility?

"Whosoever therefore shall humble himself as this little child, the same is greatest in the kingdom of heaven."

(Matthew 18:4 KJV)

But he giveth more grace. Wherefore he saith, GOD RESISTETH THE PROUD, BUT GIVETH GRACE UNTO THE HUMBLE."

(James 4:6 KJV)

"Likewise, ye younger, submit yourselves unto the elder. Yea, all of you be subject one to another, and be clothed with humility: for GOD RESISTETH THE PROUD, AND GIVETH GRACE TO THE HUMBLE."

(I Peter 5:5, 6 KJV)

"And his servants came near, and spake unto him, and said, My father, if the prophet had bid thee do some great thing, wouldest thou not have done it?

how much rather then, when he saith to thee, Wash, and be clean?"

"Then went he down, and dipped himself seven times in Jordan, according to the saying of the man of God: and his flesh came again like unto the flesh of a little child, and he was clean."

"And he returned to the man of God, he and all his company, and came, and stood before him: and he said, behold, now I know that there is no God in all the earth, but in Israel: now therefore, I pray thee, take a blessing of thy servant."

Humility is the first step toward wholeness.

(II Kings 5:13-15 KJV)

"Before destruction the heart of man is haughty; and before honour is humility."

(Proverbs 18:12 KJV)

166. What does it take to drive us from our pride into humility?

"MA-NAS'-SEH was twelve years old when he began to reign, and he reigned fifty and five years in Jerusalem:"

"But did that which was evil in the sight of the LORD, like unto the abominations of the heathen, whom the LORD had cast out before the children of Israel."

"For he built again the high places which Hez-e-ki'-ah his father had broken down, and he reared up altars for Ba'-al-im, and made grovesand worshipped all the host of heaven, and served them."

"Also he built altars in the house of the LORD, whereof the LORD had said, in Jerusalem shall my name be for ever."

"And he built altars for all the host of heaven in the two courts of the house of the LORD."

"And he caused his children to pass through the fire in the valley of the son of Hin'-nom: also he observed times, and used enchantments, and used witchcraft, and dealt with a familiar spirit, and with wizards: he wrought much evil in the sight of the LORD, to provoke him to anger."

And he set a carved image, the idol which he had made, in the house of God, of which God had said to David and to Solomon his son, In this house, and in Jerusalem, which I have chosen before all the tribes of Israel, will I put my name for ever:"

"Neither will I any more remove the foot of Israel from out of the land which I have appointed for your fathers; so that they will take heed to do all that I have commanded them, according to the whole law and the statutes and the ordinances by the hand of Moses."

"So Ma-nas'-seh made Judah and the inhabitants of Jerusalem to err, and to do worse than the heathen, whom the LORD had destroyed before the children of Israel."

"And the LORD spake to Ma-nas'-seh, and to his people; but they would not hearken."

"Wherefore the LORD brought upon them the captains of the host of the king of Assyria, which took Ma-nas'-seh among the thorns, and bound him with fetters, and carried him to Babylon."

"And when he was in affliction, he besought the LORD his God, and humbled himself greatly before the God of his fathers."

"And prayed unto him: and he was intreated of him, and heard his supplication, and brought him again to Jerusalem into his kingdom. Then Ma-nas'-seh knew that the LORD he was God."

"Now after this he built a wall without the city of David, on the west side of Gi'-hon, in the valley, even to the entering in at the fish gate, and compassed about O'-phel, and raised it up a very great height, and put captains of war in all that the fenced cities of Judah."

"And he took away the strange gods, and the idol out of the house of the LORD, and all the altars that he had built in mount of the house of the LORD, and in Jerusalem, and cast them out of the city."

Tragically, when we succeed and everything is great, we may fall into pride, thinking we have accomplished everything. However, when we are put down monetarily, physically, or in different ways, we unexpectedly think that its important to look for the Lord's help.

(II Chronicles 33:1-16 KJV)

167. Should we avoid pride even in doing God's work, the most holy and wonderful work of all?

"TAKE heed that ye do not your alms before men, to be seen of them: otherwise ye have no reward of your Father which is in heaven."

Take care! don't do your good deeds publicly, to be admired, (seen of men) because then you will lose the reward from your Father in heaven.

(Matthew 6:1 KJV)

"Serving the Lord with all humility of mind, and with many tears, and temptations, which befell me by the lying in wait of the Jews:"

I have done the Lord's work humbly-yes, and with tears.

It is anything but difficult to accomplish the Lord's work with extraordinary pride. All things considered, his work is the most superb work in all the world. In any case, Paul perceived that accomplishing God's work is serving, which takes lowliness. The individuals who are proud are bad at serving.

(Acts 20:19 KJV)

168. How will humility change our relationships with others?

"With all lowliness and meekness, with longsuffering, forbearing one another in love;"

Be humble and gentle. Be patient toward one another, offering leniency (mercy) for one another's faults in light of your love.

(Ephesians 4:2 KJV)

"And why beholdest thou the mote that is in thy brother's eye, but considered not the beam that is in thine own eye?"

Loving humility overlooks the faults of others because we see our own so clearly.

(Matthew 7:3 KJV)

PROMISE FROM GOD

"For thus saith the high and lofty One that inhabiteth eternity, whose name is Holy; I dwell in the high and holy place, with him also that is of a contrite and humble spirit, to revive the spirit of the humble, and to revive the heart of the contrite ones."

The high and grandiose (lofty) one who inhabits forever, the Holy One, says this: "I will live in that high holy place with those whose spirits are penitent and humble. I invigorate the humble and give new courage to those with repentant hearts.

(Isaiah 57:15 KJV)

INSIGNIFICANCE

169. Sometimes I look at the world and feel like my life is completely insignificant.

Does my life really matter to God?

"NOW Moses kept the flock of Je'-thro his father in law, the priest of Mid'-i-an: and he led the flock to the backside of the desert, and came to the mountain of God, even to Ho'-reb."

"And the angel of the LORD appeared unto him in a flame of fire out of the midst of a bush: and he looked, and, behold, the bush burned with fire, and the bush was not consumed."

"And Mosers said, I will now turn aside, and see this great sight, why the bush is not burnt."

"And when the LORD saw that he turned aside to see, God called unto him out of the midst of the bush, and said, Moses, Moses. And he said, Here am I."

"And God said unto Moses, I AM THAT I AM: and he said, Thus shalt thou say unto the children of Israel, I AM hath me unto you."

Moses offered very excuse in the book for why he was too insignificant to even consider doing God's work, but God saw extraordinary potential in him. Try not to keep God from working through you to achieve extraordinary or great things.

(Exodus 3:1-4: 14 KJV)

"And there came an angel of the LORD, and sat under an oak which was in Oph'-rah, that pertained unto Jo'-ash the A'-bi-ez'rite: and his son Gideon threshed wheat by the winepress, to hide it from the Mid'-i-an-ites."

"And the angel of the LORD appeared unto him, and said unto him, The LORD is with thee, thou mighty man of valour."

"And Gideon said unto him, Oh my Lord, if the LORD be for us, why then is all this befallen us? And where be all his miracles which our fathers told us of, saying, Did not the LORD bring us up from Egypt? but now the LORD hath forsaken us, and delivered us into the hands of the Mid'-i-an-ites."

"And the LORD looked upon him, and said, Go in this thy might, and thou shalt save Israel from the hand of the Mid'-i-an-ites: have not I sent thee?"

"And he said unto him, oh my Lord, wherewith shall I save Israel? Behold, my family is poor in Ma-nas'-seh, and I am the least in my father's house."

"And the LORD said unto him, Surely I will be with thee, and thou shalt smite the Mid'-i-an-ites as one man."

If God is with us, why has all this happened to us?

God can change (transform) our uncertainties and insecurities into his accomplishments.

(Judges 6:11-16 KJV)

"O LORD our Lord, how excellent is thy name in all the earth! who hast set thy glory above the heavens."

"Out of the mouth of babes and sucklings has thou ordained strength because of thine enemies, that thou mightest still the enemy and the avenger."

"When I consider thy heavens, the work of thy fingers, the moon and the stars, which thou hast ordained;"

"What is man, that thou art mindful of him? and the son of man, that thou visitest him?"

"For thou hast made him a little lower than the angels, and hast crowned him with glory and honour."

"Thou madest him to have dominion over the works of thy hands; thou hast put all things under his feet;"

"All sheep and oxen, yea, and the beasts of the field:"

"The fowl of the air, and the fish of the sea, and whatsoever passeth through the paths of the seas."

"O LORD our Lord, how excellent is thy name in all the earth!"

Despite the fact that people appear to be inconsequential (insignificant) contrasted with the inconceivability (vastness) of the universe, God loves us individually with an everlasting love.

(Psalm 8:1-9 KJV)

"For ye see your calling, brethren, how that not many wise men after the flesh, not many mighty, not many noble, are called:"

"But God hath chosen the foolish things of the world to confound the wise; and God hath chosen the weak things of the world to confound the things which are mighty;"

"And base things of the world, and things which are despised, hath God chosen, yea, and things which are not, to bring to nought things that are:"

"That no flesh should glory in his presence."

"But of him are ye in Christ Jesus, who of God is made unto us wisdom, and righteousness, and sanctification, and redemption:"

"That, according as it is written, HE THAT GLORIETH, LET HIM GLORY IN THE LORD."

Remember, dear brothers and sisters, that few of you were wise in the world's eyes, or powerful, or wealthy when God called you...

God chooses the seemingly insignificant things to reveal his power and glory.

(I Corinthians 1:26-31 KJV)

"For thou hast possessed my reins: thou hast covered me in my mother's womb."

You made all the delicate, inner parts of my body and knit me together in my mother's womb.

God made us with great skill; he crafted us with living care. He showed how much value he places on us by the way he made us.

(Psalm 139:13 KJV)

PROMISE FROM GOD

"Are not two sparrows sold for a farthing? And one of them shall not fall on the ground without your Father."

"But the very hairs of your head are all numbered."

"Fear ye not therefore, ye are of more value than many sparrows."

Not even a sparrow, worth less than a penny, can fall to the ground without your Father knowing it. And the very hairs of your head are all numbered. So don't be afraid; you are more valuable to him than a whole flock of sparrows.

(Matthew 10:29-31 KJV)

Not even a sparrow, worth less than a penny, can fall to the ground without your Father knowing it. And the very hairs of your head are all numbered. So don't be afraid; you are more valuable to him than a whole flock of sparrows.

INTIMACY

170. What does it mean to have intimacy with God?

"But his delight is in the law of the LORD; and in his law doth he meditate day and night." but they delight in doing everything the LORD wants; day and night they think about his law.

Spending time with God leads to intimacy.

(Psalm 1:2 KJV)

"Bless the LORD, O my soul: and all that is within me, bless his holy name."

"Bless the LORD, O my soul, and forget not all his benefits:"

"Who forgiveth all thine iniquities; who healeth all thy diseases;"

"Who redeemeth thy life from destruction; who crowneth thee with lovingkindness and tender mercies:"

"Who satisfieth thy mouth with good things; so that thy youth is renewed like the eagle's."

"The LORD excuteth righteousness and judgment for all that are oppressed."

"He made known his ways unto Moses, his acts unto the children of Israel."

"The LORD is merciful and gracious, slow to anger, and plenteous in mercy."

"He will not always chide: neither will he keep his anger for ever."

"He hath not dealt with us after our sins; nor rewarded us according to our iniquities."

"For as the heaven is high above he earth, so great is his mercy toward them that fear him."

"As far as the east is from the west, so far hath he removed our transgressions from us."

"Like as a father pitieth his children, so the LORD pitieth them that fear him."

"For he knoweth our frame; he remembereth that we are dust."

"As for man, his days are as grass: as a flower of the field, so he flourisheth."

"For the wind passeth over it, and it is gone; and the place thereof shall know it no more."

"But the mercy of the LORD is from everlasting to everlasting upn them that fear him, and his righteousness unto children's children;"

"To such as keep has covenant, and to those that remember his commandments to do them."

"The LORD hath prepared his throne in the heavens; and his kingdom ruleth over all."

"Bless the LORD, ye his angels, that excel in strength, that do his commandments, hearkening unto the voice of his word."

"Bless ye the LORD, all ye his hosts; ye ministers of his, that do his pleasure."

"Bless the LORD, all his works in all places of his dominion: bless the LORD, O my soul."

God's unfailing love is as great as the heights of the heavens above the earth.

This whole psalm describes how we can have an intimate relationship with God.

(Psalm 103:1-22 KJV)

"And it shall be at that day, saith the LORD, that thou shalt call me Ish'-i; and shalt call me no more Ba'-al-i."

"For I will take away the name of Ba'-al-im out of her mouth, and they shall no more be remembered by their name."

"And in that day will I make a covenant for them with the beasts of the field, and with the fowls of heaven, and with the creeping things of the ground: and I will break the bow and the sword and the battle out of the earth, and will make them to lie down safely."

"And I will betroth thee unto me for ever; yea, I will betroth thee unto me in righteousness, and in judgment, and in lovingkindness, and in mercies."

"I will even betroth thee unto me in faithfulness: and thou shalt know the LORD."

(Hosea 2:16-20 KJV)

"Behold, what manner of love the Father hath bestowed upon us, that we should be called the sons of God: therefore the world knoweth us not, because it knew him not."

God reaches out to us, offering an intimate relationship-as intimate as husband and wife or father and child, a commitment that is forever, a love relationship such as we have never known before.

(I John 3:1 KJV)

"Blessed are the poor in heart: for they shall see God."

Intimacy means coming to God with a clean heart and pure motives.

(Matthew 5:8 KJV)

"The LORD THY God in the midst of thee is mighty; he will save, he will rejoice over thee with joy; he will rest in his love, he will joy over thee with singing."

God has arrived to live among you...He will exult over you by singing a happy song.

The Lord God, Creator of the universe, singing songs about you! What a portrait of a living intimate God.

(Zephaniah 3:17 KJV)

"And, behold, I am with thee, and will keep thee in all places whither thou goest, and will bring thee again into this land; for I will not leave thee, until I have done that which I spoken to thee of."

(Genesis 28:15 KJV)

"And he said, My presence shall go with thee, and I will give thee rest." I will personally go with you.

(Exodus 33:14 KJV)

"The LORD is my shepherd; I shall not want."

"He maketh me to lie down in green pastures: he leadeth me beside the still waters."

"He restoreth my soul: he leadeth me in the paths of righteousness for his name's sake."

"Yea, though I walk through the valley of the shadow of death, I will fear no evil: for thou art with me; they rod and thy staff they comfort me."

"Thou preparest a table before me in the presence of mine enemies: thou anointest my head with oil; my cup runneth over."

"Surely goodness and mercy shall follow me all the days of my life: and I will dwell in the house of the LORD for ever."

The Lord is my shepherd.

(Psalm 23:1-6 KJV)

"Teaching them to observe all things whatsoever I have commanded you: and, lo, I am with you always, even unto the end of the world."

The Lord is with us, as close as we want him to be, as long as we let him be, until the end of life.

There are vows of permanent intimacy with us.

(Matthew 28:20 KJV)

171. What is the basis for true and lasting intimacy in marriage?

"Drink waters out of thine own cistern, and running waters out of thine own well."

"Let thy fountains be dispersed abroad, and rivers of waters in the streets."

"Let them be only thine own, and not strangers' with thee."

"Let thy fountain be blessed: and rejoice with the wife of thy youth."

"Let her be as the loving hind and pleasant roe; let her breasts satisfy thee at all times; and be thou ravished always with her love."

Drink water from your own well-share your love only with your wife...May you always be captivated by her love.

(Proverbs 5:15-19 KJV)

"Whoso findeth a wife findeth a good thing, and obtaineth favour of the LORD."

A man who finds a wife finds a treasure.

(Proverbs 18:22 KJV)

"Who can find a virtuous woman? For her price is far above rubies."

"The heart of her husband doth safely trust in her, so that he shall have no need of spoil."

"She will do him good and not evil all the days of her life."

"Who can locate an upright and skilled wife? She is worth more than valuable rubies.

Her husband can trust in her, and she will greatly enrich his life.

(Proverbs 31:10-12 KJV)

"Let the husband render unto the wife due benevolence; and likewise also the wife unto the husband."

"The wife hath not power of her own body, but the husband: and likewise also the husband hath not power of his own body, but the wife."

"Defraud ye not one the other except it be with consent for a time that ye may give yourselves to fasting and prayer; and come together again that Satan tempt you not for your incontinency."

(I Corinthians 7:3- KJV 5)

"Wives, submit yourselves unto your own husbands, as unto the Lord."

"For the husband is the head of the wife, even as Christ is the head of the church; and he is the saviour of the body."

"Therefore as the church is subject unto Christ, so let the wives be to their own husbands in every thing."

"Husbands, love your wives, even as Christ also loved the church, and gave himself for it;"

"That he might sanctify and cleanse it with the washing of water by the word,"

"That he might present it to himself a glorious church, not having spot, or wrinkle, or any such thing; but that it should be holy and without blemish."

"So ought men to love their wives as their own bodies. He that loveth his wife loveth himself."

"For no man ever yet hated his own flesh; but nourisheth and cherisheth it, even as the Lord the church:"

"For we are members of his body, of his flesh, and of his bones."

"FOR THIS CAUSE SHALL A MAN LEAVE HIS FATHER AND MOTHER, AND SHALL BE JOINED UNTO HIS WIFE, AND THEY TWO SHALL BE ONE FLESH."

"This is a great mystery: but I speak concerning Christ and the church."

"Nevertheless let every one of you in particular so love his wife even as himself; and the wife see that she reverence her husband."

True and lasting intimacy in marriage is based upon the following:

(1) faithfulness;
(2) rejoicing in one another;
(3) letting each satisfy the other in love and sexuality;
(4) accepting one's mate as a blessing from the Lord;
(5) recognizing the great value of one's mate;
(6) recognizing how much one's mate can truly bring delight and satisfaction;
(7) living happily with each other;
(8) talking together about the Lord and spiritual things;
(9) giving thanks to the Lord together;;
(10) submitting to each other;
(11) loving each other as passionately as Christ loved the church and died for it.

(Ephesians 5:22-33 KJV)

PROMISE FROM GOD

"And thou, Solomon my son, know thou the God of thy father, and serve him with a perfect heart and with a willing mind: for the LORD searcheth all hearts, and understandeth all the imaginations of the thoughts: if thou seek him, he will be found of thee; but if thou forsake him, he will cast thee off for ever."

Worship and serve him with your whole heart and with a willing mind. For the LORD sees every heart and understands and knows every plan and thought. If you seek him, you will find him….

(I Chronicles 28:9 KJV)

JEALOUSY

172. Why is our jealousy so dangerous?

"A sound heart is the life of the flesh: but envy the rottenness of the bones."

Jealousy can bring decay to our lives because it causes us to focus on anger and bitterness.

(Proverbs 14:30 KJV)

"Wrath is cruel, and anger is outrageous; but who is able to stand before envy?"

(Proverbs 27:4 KJV)

"And there was a strife between the herdmen of Abram's cattle and he herdmen of Lot's cattle; and the Ca'-naan-ite and the Per'-iz-zite dwelled then in the land."

Jealousy can tear families and friends apart. Jealousy drove Lot's herdsmen to fight with his uncle Abram's herdsmen.

(Genesis 13:7 KJV)

173. What does it mean that God is "a jealous God"?

"For thou shalt worship no other god: for the LORD, whose name is Jealous, is a jealous God:"

(Exodus 34:14 KJV)

"Thou shalt not bow down thyself unto them, nor serve them: for I am the LORD thy God am a jealous God, visiting the iniquity of the fathers upon the children unto the third and fourth generation of them that hate me,"

I am a jealous God and you will not share you love with any other god.

(Deuteronomy 5:9 KJV)

"They have moved me to jealousy with that which is not God; they have provoked me to anger with their vanities: and I will move them to jealousy with those which are not a people; I will provoke them to anger with a foolish nation."

(Deuteronomy 32:21 KJV)

"So the angel that communed with me said unto me, Cry thou, saying, Thus saith the LORD of hosts; I am jealous for Jerusalem and for Zion with a great jealousy."

When people give their respect, honor, commendation (praise), and love to other things, God is jealous that the respect, the honor due him has been wasted somewhere else. Since God merits all our respect, praise, and love, this is a fair acknowledgment of what he deserves.

(Zechariah 1:14 KJV)

174. Where does jealousy take us? What can happen next?

"The wicked desireth the net of evil men: but the root of the righteous yielded fruit."

Thieves are jealous of each other's loot, while the godly bear their own fruit.

Thieves take from others because of their jealousy (lust) and desire for another person's cash. Generous individuals, on the other hand, love to give and that turns into their main impetus throughout everyday life.

(Proverbs 12:12 KJV)

"And Abel, he also brought of the firstlings of his flock and of the fat thereof. And the LORD had respect unto Abel and to his offering."

"But unto Cain and to his offering he had not respect. And Cain was very wroth, and his countenance fell."

"And the LORD said unto Cain, Why art thou wroth? and why is thy countenance fallen?"

"If thou doest well, shalt thou not be accepted? and if thou doest not well, sin lieth at the door. And unto thee shall be his desire, and thou shalt rule over him."

"And Cain talked with Abel his brother: and it came to pass, when they were in the field, that Cain rose up against Abel his brother, and slew him."

The LORD accepted Abel's offering, but he did not accept Cain's. This made Cain very angry..

(Genesis 4:4-8 KJV)

"But the fruit of the Spirit is love, joy, peace, longsuffering, gentleness, goodness, faith,"

"Meekness, temperance: against such there is no law."

"And they that are Christ's have crucified the flesh with the afflections and lusts."

"If we live in the Spirit, let us also walk in the Spirit."

"Let us not be desirous of vain glory, provoking one another, envying one another."

When we look for the character traits that originate from the Holy Spirit, we are saved from negligible human desire of jealousy and the hard sentiments that originate from the composition for honor and popularity.

(Galatians 5:22-26 KJV)

PROMISE FROM GOD

"Therefore I say unto you, What things soever ye desire, when ye pray, believe that ye receive them, and ye shall have them."

"And when ye stand praying, forgive, if ye have ought against any: that your Father also which is in heaven may forgive you your trespasses."

Listen to me! You can pray to God for anything, and in the event that you accept, you will have it. However, when you are praying, first forgive anybody you are holding resentment against, with the goal that your Father in paradise will forgive your transgressions, as well.

(Mark 11:24, 25 KJV)

JUSTICE

175. Is God always fair and just?

"O LORD, rebuke me not in thine anger, neither chasten me in thy hot displeasure."

"Have mercy upon me, O LORD; for I am weak: O LORD, heal me; for my bones are vexed."

"My soul is also sore vexed: but thou, O LORD, how long?"

(Psalm 6:1-3 KJV)

"O LORD God of Israel, thou art righteous: for we remain yet escaped, as it is this day: behold, we are before thee in our trespasses: for we cannot stand before thee because of this."

We ask God not for justice, lest he punish us, but to feel sorry for us (pity), so he will forgive us. We ask God, not for fairness, lest he bring judgment, but for mercy, so it won't.

(Ezra 9:15 KJV)

"Which is a manifest token of the righteous judgment of God, that ye may be counted worthy of the kingdom of God, for which ye also suffer:"

"Seeing it is a righteous thing with God to recompense tribulation to them that trouble you;"

When you are troubled with inconveniences or troubles, it is tempting to imagine that God isn't reasonable or just. By what method would God be able to permit a Christian to suffer when such a large number of unbelievers down the road are prospering? Yet, have faith that God's justice will prevail.

(II Thessalonians 1:5, 6 KJV)

"Thou shalt not rise a false report: put not thine hand with the wicked to be an unrighteous witness."

"Thou shalt not follow a multitude to do evil; neither shalt thou speak in a cause to decline after many to wrest judgment:"

"Neither shalt thou countenance a poor man in his cause."

Do not pass along false reports. Do not cooperate with evil people...do not slant your testimony.

(Exodus 23:1-3 KJV)

"If ye love me, keep my commandments."

(John 14:15 KJV)

"But let judgment run down as waters, and righteousness as a mighty stream."

We pursue justice out of our love for God, who commands us to be just.

(Amos 5:24 KJV)

"And I saw the dead, small and great, stand before God; and the books were opened: and another book was opened, which is the book of life: and the dead were judged out of those things which were written in the books, according to their works."

"And the sea gave up the dead which were in it; and death and hell delivered up the dead which were in them: and they were judged every man according to their works."

"And death and hell were cast into the lake of fire. This is the second death."

"And whosoever was not found written in the book of life was cast into the lake of fire."

God rewards those who seek after justice.

(Revelation 20:12-15 KJV)

"Jesus saith unto him, I am the way, the truth, and the life: no man cometh unto the Father, but by me."

God didn't simply create truth, he is Truth itself. If we need to live for God, we must maintain truth no matter what and at all costs or we will end up being an accessory to foul play (injustice).

(John 14:6 KJV)

176. What should I do when justice is abused?

"Defend the poor and fatherless: do justice to the afflicted and needy."

Speak out against injustice.

(Psalm 82:3 KJV)

"Break their teeth, O God, in their mouth: break out the great teeth of the young lions, O LORD."

"Let them melt away as waters which run continually: when he bendeth his bow to shoot his arrows, let them be as cut in pieces."

Pray that God would intervene.

(Psalm 58: 6, 7 KJV)

"THUS saith the LORD, keep ye judgment, and do justice: for my salvation is near to come, and my righteousness to be revealed."

Be just and fair to all, say the LORD. Do what is right and good.

(Isaiah 56:1 KJV)

"Render therefore to all their dues: tribute to whom tribute is due; custom to whom custom; fear to whom fear; honour to whom honour."

Render or give everyone what you owe them.

(Romans 13:7 KJV)

"Say not thou, I will recompense evil; but wait on the LORD, and he shall save thee."

Do not repay evil with evil. Don't seek revenge.

(Proverbs 20:22 KJV)

177. How do God's justice and mercy relate?

"And the LORD spake unto Moses, saying,"

"Speak unto the children of Israel, and say unto them, When ye be come over Jordan into the land of Canaan;"

"Then ye shall appoint you cities to be cities of refuge for you; that the slayer may flee thither, which killeth any person at unawares."

"And they shall be unto you cities for refuge from the avenger; that the manslayer die not, until he stand before the congregation in judgment."

"And of these cities which ye shall give six cities shall ye have for refuge."

"Ye shall give three cities on this side Jordan, and three cities shall ye give in the land of Canaan, which shall be cities of refuge."

"These six cities shall be a refuge, both for the children of Israel, and for the stranger, and for the sojourner among them: that every one that killeth any person unawares may flee thither."

"And if he smite him with an instrument of iron, so that he die, he is a murderer: the murderer shall surely be put to death."

"And if he smite him with throwing a stone, wherewith he may die, and he die, he is a murderer: the murderer shall surely be put to death."

"Or if he smite him with an hand weapon of wood, wherewith he may die, and he die, he is a murderer: the murderer shall surely be put to death."

"The revenger of blood himself shall slay the murderer: when he meeteth him, he shall slay him."

"But if he thrust him of hatred, or hurl at him by laying of wait, that he die:"

"Or in enmity smite him with his hand, that he die: he that smote him shall surely be put to death; for he is a murderer: the revenger of blood shall slay the murderer, when he meeteth him."

"But if he thrust him suddenly without enmity, or have cast upon him any thing without laying of wait,"

"Or with any stone, wherewith a man may die, seeing him not, and cast it upon him, that he die, and was not his enemy, neither sought his harm:"

"Then the congregation shall judge between the slayer and the revenger of blood according to these judgments:"

"And the congregation shall deliver the slayer out of the hand of the revenger of blood, and the congregation shall restore him to the city of his refuge, whither he was fled: and he shall abide in it unto the death of the high priest, which was anointed with the holy oil."

And the Lord said unto Moses….designate cities of refuge for people to flee to...

(Numbers 35:9-25 KJV)

"And David said unto Gad, I am in a great strait: let us fall now into the hand of the LORD; for his mercies are great: and let me not fall into the hand of man."

(II Samuel 24:14 KJV)

"For the wages of sin is death; but the gift of God is eternal life through Jesus Christ our Lord."

God is just in that he plainly tells to us what sin is and what its consequences will be. All people are dealt with equally. God is tolerant in that he offers a route for us to be saved the punishment we deserve for our transgression (sins). We would be in much worse shape if we always got the justice we deserved.

(Romans 6:23 KJV)

"Ye have heard that it hath been said, THOU SHALT LOVE THY NEIGHBOUR, and hate thine enemy."

"But I say unto you, Love your enemies, bless them that curse you, do good to them which despitefully use you, and persecute you;"

That ye may be the children of your Father which is in heaven: for he maketh his sun to rise on the evil and on the good, and sendeth rain on the just and on the unjust."

Justice rebuffs insidiousness, wrongdoing, and bad behavior. Mercy forgives them. Perhaps the hardest thing we can do is forgive somebody who has wronged us. In any case, it is just through experiencing forgiveness that one can clearly see God's extraordinary gift of salvation. Your mercy might be exactly what somebody needs to be guided (ushered) into God's kingdom.

(Matthew 5:43-45 KJV)

PROMISE FROM GOD

"So that a man shall say, Verily there is a reward for the righteous: verily he is a God that judgeth in the earth."

Then at last everyone will say, "There truly is a reward for those who live for God; surely there is a God who judges justly here on earth."

(Psalm 58:11 KJV)

KINDNESS

178. Why should we be kind to one another?

"And be ye kind one to another, tenderhearted, forgiving one another, even as God for Christ's sake hath forgiven you."

We should be kind because God has been kind to us and commands us to be kind to others.

(Ephesians 4:32 KJV)

"Therefore all things whatsoever ye would that men should do to you, do ye even so to them: for this is the law and the prophets."

We're kind because we want others to be kind to us.

(Matthew 7:12 KJV)

"Then she fell on her face, and bowed herself to the ground, and said unto him, Why have I found grace in thine eyes, that thou shouldest take knowledge of me, seeing I am a stranger?"

"And Boaz answered and said unto her, It hath fully been shewed me, all that thou hast done unto thy mother in law since the death of thine husband: and how thou hast left thy father and they mother, and the land of thy nativity, and art come unto a people which thou knewest not heretofore."

"The LORD recompense thy work, and a full reward be given thee of the LORD God of Israel, under whose wings thou art come to trust."

(Ruth 2:10-12 KJV)

179. Where do we get Christian kindness?

"But the fruit of the Spirit is love, joy, peace, longsuffering, gentleness, goodness, faith,"

Kindness is a fruit that comes from the Holy Spirit planted within us.

(Galatians 5:22 KJV)

"Charity suffereth long, and is kind; charity envieth not; charity vaunteth not itself, is not puffed up."

From the foundations of love flow the rivers of kindness. It is impossible to be truly kind unless we are first truly loving.

(I Corinthians 13:4 KJV)

"But love ye your enemies, and do good, and lend, hoping for nothing again: and your reward shall be great, and ye shall be the children of the Highest: for he is kind unto the unthankful and to the evil."

Kindness is based on the loving heart of the giver, not the loving heart of the recipient.

(Luke 6:35 KJV)

180. How do we show God our gratitude for his kindness?

"To shew forth thy lovingkindness in the morning, and thy faithfulness every night."

We must remember daily to thank and praise the Lord for his kindness and faithfulness!

(Psalm 92:2 KJV)

181. How has God shown kindness to us?

"But after that the kindness and love of God our Saviour toward man appeared,"

"Not by works of righteousness which we have done, but according to his mercy he saved us, by the washing of regeneration, and renewing of the Holy Ghost;"

"Which he shed on us abundantly through Jesus Christ our Saviour;"

God our Savior gave us his kindness and love. He saved us, not as a result of the good things we did, but because of his mercy. He washed away our transgressions (sins) which he shed on us through Jesus Christ our Savior.

(Titus 3:4-6 KJV)

PROMISE FROM GOD

"And whosoever shall give to drink unto one of these little ones a cup of cold water only in the name of a disciple, verily I say unto you, he shall in no wise lose his reward."

If you even give a cup of cold water to one of the least of my followers, you will surely be rewarded.

(Matthew 10:42 KJV)

LEADERSHIP

182. What are some qualities of a good leader?

"THIS is a true saying, If a man desire the office of a bishop, he desireth a good work."

"A bishop then must be blameless, the husband of one wife, vigilant, sober, of good behaviour, given to hospitality, apt to teach;"

"Not given to wine, no striker, not greedy of filthy lucre; but patient, not a brawler, not covetous;"

"One that ruleth well his own house, having his children in subjection with all gravity;"

"(For if a man know not how to rule his own house, how shall he take care of the church of God?)"

"Not a novice, lest being lifted up with pride he fall into the condemnation of the devil."

"Moreover he must have a good report of them which are without; lest he fall into reproach and the snare of the devil."

"Likewise must the deacons be grave, not doubttongued, not given to much wine, not greedy of filthy lucre;"

"Holding the mystery of the faith in a pure conscience."

"And let these also first be proved; then let them use the office of a deacon, being found blameless."

"Even so must their wives be grave, not slanderers, sober, faithful in all things."

"Let the deacons be the husbands of one wife, ruling their children and their own houses well."

An elder must be a man whose life can not be spoken against.

(I Timothy 3:1-12 KJV)

"If any be blameless, the husband of one wife, having faithful children not accused of riot or unruly."

"For a bishop must be blameless, as the steward of God; not self-willed, not soon angry, not given to wine, no striker, not given to filthy lucre;"

"But a lover of hospitality, a lover of good men, sober, just, holy, temperate;"

In these verses Paul shows us many characteristics for anyone in church leadership.

(Titus 1:6-9 KJV)

"That I gave my brother Ha-na'-ni, and Han-a-ni'-ah the ruler of the palace, charge over

Jerusalem: for he was a faithful man, and feared God above many."

Good leaders display faithfulness and reverence.

(Nehemiah 7:2 KJV)

"But it shall not be so among you; but whosoever will be great among you, let him be your minister;"

Good leaders have a servant's heart.

(Matthew 20:26 KJV)

"And for this cause Hez-e-ki'-ah the king, and the prophet Isaiah the son of Amoz, prayed and cried to heaven."

A good leader has a heart for prayer.

(II Chronicles 32:20 KJV)

“And David said unto God, I have sinned greatly, because I have done this thing: but now, I beseech thee, do away the iniquity of thy servant; for I have done very foolishly.”

Good leaders accept responsibility for their actions.

(I Chronicles 21:8 KJV)

“According to the grace of God which is given unto me, as a wise masterbuilder, I have laid the foundation, and another buildeth thereon. But let every man take heed how he buildeth thereupon.”

“For other foundation can no man lay than that is laid, which is Jesus Christ.”

“Now if any man build upon this foundation gold, silver, precious stones, wood, hay, stubble;”

“Every man’s work shall be made manifest: for the day shall declare it, because it shall be revealed by fire; and the fire shall try every man’s work of what sort it is.”

"If any man's work abide which he hath built thereupon, he shall receive a reward."

"If any man's work shall be burned, he shall suffer loss: but he himself shall be saved; yet so as by fire."

Good leaders keep their eyes on Jesus Christ.

(I Corinthians 3:10-15 KJV)

"Now when Daniel knew that the writing was signed, he went into his house; and his windows being open in his chamber toward Jerusalem, he kneeled upon his knees three times a day, and prayed, and gave thanks before his God, as he did aforetime."

The words and actions of a good leader are consistent. Daniel was vocal about his faith in God, even in a pagan land, and his actions backed that up.

Good leaders need courage based on the assurance of God's presence.

(Daniel 6:10 KJV)

"He must increase, but I must decrease."

Good leaders do no emphasize themselves.

(John 3:30 KJV)

“BELOVED, believe not every spirit, but try the spirits whether they are of God: because many false prophets are gone out into the world.”

Beloved, Do not believe everyone who claims to speak by the Spirit.

(I John 4:1) KJV

“If there come any unto you, and bring not this doctrine, receive him not into your house, neither bid him God speed:”

If someone comes to your meeting and does not teach the truth about Christ, don’t encourage him in any way.

Good leaders recognize false teaching and boldly combat it.

(II John 1:10 KJV)

“AND I said, Hear, I pray you, O heads of Jacob, and ye princes of the house of Israel;

Is it not for you to know judgment?”

“Who hate the good, and love the evil; who pluck off their skin from off them, and their flesh from off their bones;”

"Who also eat the flesh of my people, and flay their skin from off them; and they break their bones, and chop them into pieces, as for the pot, and as flesh within the caldron."

"Then shall they cry unto the LORD, but he will not hear them: he will even hide his face from them at that time, as they have behaved themselves ill in their doings."

"Thus saith the LORD concerning the prophets that make my people err, that bite with their teeth, and cry, Peace; and he that putteth not into their mouths, they even prepare war against him."

"Therefore night shall be unto you, that ye shall not have a vision; and it shall be dark unto you, that ye shall not divine; and the sun shall go down over the prophets, and the day shall be dark over them."

"Then shall the seers be ashamed, and the diviners confounded: yea, they shall all cover their lips; for there is no answer of God."

"But truly I am full of power by the spirit of the LORD, and of judgment, and of might, to declare unto Jacob his transgression, and to Israel his sin."

"Hear this, I pray you, ye heads of the house of Jacob, and princes of the house of Israel, that abhor judgment, and pervert all equity."

"They build up Zion with blood, and Jerusalem with iniquity."

"The heads thereof judge for reward, and the priests thereof teach for hire, and the prophets thereof divine for money: yet will they lean upon the LORD, and say, Is not the LORD among us? none evil can come upon us."

Good leaders are consumed with doing what is right.

(Micah 3:1-11 KJV)

"THEREFORE leaving the principles of the doctrine of Christ, let us go on unto perfection; not laying again the foundation of repentance from dead works, and of faith toward God,"

Let us go on instead and become mature in our understanding.

Good leaders display maturity, both in their activities and in their insight (knowledge) into God's word.

(Hebrews 6:1 KJV)

"NOW these are they that came to David to Zik'-lag, while he yet kept himself close because of Saul the son of Kish: and they were among the mighty men, helpers of the war."

"They were armed with bows, and could use both the right hand and the left in hurling stones and shooting arrows out of a bow, even of Saul's brethren of Benjamin."

Good leaders are not undermined (threatened) by skilled subordinates. They gather skilled people around them.

(I Chronicles 12:1, 2 KJV)

"The way of a fool is right in his own eyes: but he that hearkeneth unto counsel is wise."

Fools think they need no advice, but the wise listen to others.

Good leaders have others who hold them accountable.

(Proverbs 12:15 KJV)

183. How do we go about choosing a good leader?

"But the LORD said unto Samuel, Look not on his countenance, or on the height of his stature; because I have refused him: for the LORD seeth not as man seeth; for man looketh on the outward appearance, but the LORD looketh on the heart."

Look for qualities of a good leader listed in the previous question #182. Don't be swayed by physical appearance, but look deep into the person's heart.

(I Samuel 16:7 KJV)

184. How should we treat our leaders?

"Obey them that have the rule over you, and submit yourselves: for they watch for your souls, as they that must give account, that they may do it with joy, and not with grief: for that is unprofitable for you."

The work of our spiritual leaders is to watch over our souls. We must obey our spiritual leaders and do what they say.

(Hebrews 13:17 KJV)

“LET every soul be subject unto the higher powers. For there is no power but of God: the powers that be are ordained of God.”

“Whosoever therefore resisteth the power, resisteth the ordinance of God: and they that resist shall receive to themselves damnation.”

“For rulers are not a terror to good works, but to the evil. Wilt thou then not be afraid of the power? do that which is good, and thou shall have praise of the same:”

“For he is the minister of God to thee for good. But if thou do that which is evil, be afraid; for he beareth not the sword in vain: for he is the minister of God, a revenger to execute wrath upon him that doeth evil.”

“Wherefore ye must needs be subject, not only for wrath, but also for conscience sake.”

Obey our government, for God is the one who put it there…

Work with leaders rather than against them to effect change.

(Romans 13:1-5 KJV)

"And we beseech you, brethren, to know them which labour among you, and are over you in the Lord, and admonish you;"

"And to esteem them very highly in love for their work's sake. And be at peace among yourselves.

Honor the individuals who are your leaders in the Lord's work...Think profoundly (highly) of them and give them your wholehearted love on account of their work.

(I Thessalonians 5:12, 13 KJV)

"So Joshua did as Moses had said to him, and fought with Am'-a-lek: and Moses, Aaron, and Hur went up to the top of the hill."

"And it came to pass, when Moses held up his hand, that Israel prevailed: and when he let down his hand, Am'-a-lek prevailed."

"But Moses' hands were heavy; and they took a stone, and put it under him, and he sat thereon; and Aaron and Hur stayed up his hands, the one on the one side, and the other on the other side; and his hands were steady until the going down of the sun."

"And Joshua discomfited Am'-a-lek and his people with the edge of the sword."

Encourage them!

(Exodus 17:10-13 KJV)

"Pray for us: for we trust we have a good conscience, in all things willing to live honestly."

"But I beseech you the rather to do this, that I may be restored to you the sooner."

Pray for us..I especially need your prayers right now.

Pray for them.

(Hebrews 13:18, 19 KJV)

"But why dost thou judge thy brother? or why dost thou set at nought thy brother? for we shall all stand before the judgment seat of Christ."

Why do you condemn another Christian? Why do you look down on another Christian?

Don't be too quick to criticize

(Romans 14:10 KJV)

"AND the LORD sent Nathan unto David. And he came unto him, and said unto him, There were two men in one city; the one rich, and the other poor."

"The rich man had exceeding many flocks and herds:"

"But the poor man had nothing, save one little ewe lamb, which he had bought and nourished up: and it grew up together with him, and with his children; it did eat of his own meat, and drank of his own cup, and lay in his bosom, and was unto him as a daughter."

And there came a traveller unto the rich man, and he spared to take of his own flock and of his own herd, to dress for the wayfaring man that was come unto him; but took the poor man's lamb, and dressed it for the man that was come to him."

"And David's anger was greatly kindled against the man; and he said to Natrhan, As the LORD liveth, the man that hath done this thing shall surely die:"

"And he shall restore the lamb fourfold, because he did this thing, and because he had no pity."

"And Nathan said to David, Thou art the man. Thus saith the LORD God of Israel, I anointed thee king over Israel, and I delivered thee out of the hand of Saul;"

"And I gave thee thy master's house, and thy master's wives into thy bosom, and gave thee the house of Israel and of Judah; and if that had been too little, I would moreover have given unto thee such and such things."

Wherefore hast thou despised the commandment of the LORD, to do evil in his sight? thou hast killed U-ri'-ah the Hit'-tite with the sword, and hast taken his wife to be thy wife, and hast slain him with the sword of the children of Ammon."

"Now therefore the sword shall never depart from thine house; because thou hast despised me, and hast taken the wife of U-ri'-ah the Hit'-tite to be thy wife."

"Thus saith the LORD, Behold, I will raise up evil against thee out of thine own house, and I will take thy wives before thine eyes, and give them unto thy neighbour, and he shall lie with thy wives in the sight of this sun."

"For thou didst it secretly: but I will do this thing before all Israel, and before the sun."

"And David said unto Nathan, I have sinned against the LORD, And Nathan said unto David, The LORD also hath put away thy sin; thou shalt not die."

Hold them accountable.

(II Samuel 12:1-13 KJV)

PROMISE FROM GOD

"Have not I commanded thee? Be strong and of a good courage; be not afraid, neither be thou dismayed: for the LORD thy God is with thee whithersoever thou goest."

....be strong and courageous!...For the LORD your God is with you wherever you go!

(Joshua 1:9 KJV)

LISTENING

185. Why is listening so important?

"My son, hear the instruction of thy father, and forsake not the law of thy mother:"

"For they shall be an ornament of grace unto thy head, and chains about thy neck."

Listening helps us grow and mature.

(Proverbs 1:8, 9 KJV)

“And have not obeyed the voice of my teachers, nor inclined mine ear to them that instructed me!”

Listening helps keep us accountable.

(Proverbs 5:13 KJV)

“MY son, if thou wilt receive my words, and hide my commandments with thee;”

“So that thou incline thine ear unto wisdom, and apply thine heart to understanding;”

“Yea, if thou criest after knowledge, and liftest up thy voice for understanding;”

“If thou seekest her as silver, and searchest for her as for hid treasures;”

“Then shalt thou understand the fear of the LORD, and find the knowledge of God.”

“For the LORD giveth wisdom: out of his mouth cometh knowledge and understanding.”

"He layeth up sound wisdom for the righteous; he is a buckler to them that walk uprightly."

"He keepeth the paths of judgment, and preserveth the way of his saints."

Then shalt thou understand righteousness, and judgment, and equity; yea, every good path."

My child, listen to me...Then ...you will know how to find the right course of action every time.

Listening is essential to good decision making.

(Proverbs 2:1-9 KJV)

"DOTH not wisdom cry? and understanding put forth her voice?"

"She standeth in the top of high places, by the way in the places of the path."

"She crieth at the gates, at the entry of the city, at the coming in at the doors."

"Unto you, O men, I call; and my voice is to the sons of man."

"O ye simple, understand wisdom; and, ye fools, be ye of an understanding heart."

“Hear; for I will speak of excellent things; and the opening of my lips shall be right things.”

“For my mouth shall speak truth; and wickedness is an abomination to my lips.”

“All the words of my mouth are in righteousness; there is nothing froward or perverse in them.”

“They are all plain to him that understandeth, and right to them that find knowledge.”

“Receive my instruction, and not silver; and knowledge rather than choice gold.”

“For wisdom is better than rubies; and all the things that may be desired are not to be compared to it,”

“I wisdom dwell with prudence, and find out knowledge of witty inventions.”

Listening keeps us from being closed minded.

(Proverbs 8:1-12 KJV)

“So Moses hearkened to the voice of his father in law, and did all that he had said.”

Moses listened to his father in law's advice and followed his suggestions.

(Exodus 18:24 KJV)

"Unto me men gave ear, and waited, and kept silence at my counsel."

"After my words they spake not again; and my speech dropped upon them."

"And they waited for me as for the rain; and they opened their mouth wide as for the latter rain."

Listening shows that we regard others. It respects the expressions of others.

There is something affirming about feeling that you've been listened to.

(Job 29:21-23 KJV)

"Whoso stoppeth his ears at the cry of the poor, he also shall cry himself, but shall not be heard."

Those who shut their ears to the cries of the poor will be ignored in their own time of need.

Listening is more than hearing; it's an interfacing with others. It encourages us know what they are accustomed to (where they are coming from).

(Proverbs 21:13 KJV)

186. What are some things we shouldn't listen to?

"NOW the serpent was more subtil than any beast of the field which the LORD God had made. And he said unto the woman, Yea, hath God said, Ye shall not eat of every tree of the garden?"

"And the woman said unto the serpent, We may eat of the fruit of the trees of the garden:"

"But of the fruit of the tree which is in the midst of the garden, God hath said, Ye shall not eat of it, neither shall ye touch it, lest ye die."

"And the serpent said unto the woman, Ye shall not surely die:"

"For God doth know that in the day ye eat thereof, then your eyes shall be opened, and ye shall be as gods, knowing good and evil."

"And when the woman saw that the tree was good for food, and that it was pleasant to the eyes, and a tree to be desired to make one wise, she took of the fruit thereof, and did eat, and gave also unto her husband with her; and he did eat."

The fruit looked so fresh and delicious...So she did eat. and her husband did also.

(Genesis 3:1-6 KJV)

"And lead us not into temptation, but deliver us from evil: For thine is the kingdom, and the power, and the glory, for ever. A-men."

And don't let us yield to temptation...

(Matthew 6:13 KJV)

"Thou shalt not go up and down as a talebearer among thy people: neither shalt thou stand against the blood of thy neighbour: I am the LORD."

Do not spread slanderous expressions or gossip among your people.

(Leviticus 19:16 KJV)

"BUT there were false prophets also among the people, even as there shall be false teachers among you, who privily shall bring in damnable heresies, even denying the

Lord that bought them, and bring upon themselves swift destruction."

"And many shall follow their pernicious ways; by reason of whom the way of truth shall be evil spoken of."

"And through covetousness shall they with feigned words make merchandise of you: whose judgment now of a long time lingereth not, and their damnation slumbereth not."

Just as there were false prophets in Israel, there will be false teachers among you.

(II Peter 2:1-3 KJV)

"And then if any man shall say to you, Lo, here is Christ; or, lo, he is there; believe him not:"

"For false Christs and false prophets shall rise, and shall shew signs and wonders, to seduce, if it were possible, even the elect."

"But take ye heed: behold, I have foretold you all things."

And then if anyone tells you, "Look, here is the Messiah," or "There he is," don't believe it, for it is "False Teaching."

(Mark 13:21-23 KJV)

"Neither filthiness, nor foolish talking, nor jesting, which are not convenient: but rather giving of thanks."

Obscene stories, foolish talk, and coarse jokes-these are not for you.

(Ephesians 5:4 KJV)

"There is that speaketh like the piercing of a sword: but the tongue of the wise is health."

Some people make cutting remarks, but the words of the wise bring healing.

Insults and off-color stories.

(Proverbs 12:18 KJV)

"A righteous man hateth lying: but a wicked man is loathsome, and cometh to shame."

Those who are godly hate lies.

(Proverbs 13:5 KJV)

"A man that flattereth his neighbour spreadeth a net for his feet."

To flatter people is to lay a trap for their feet.

Flattery.

(Proverbs 29:5 KJV)

187. How do we listen to God?

"But know that the LORD hath set apart him that is godly for himself: the LORD will hear when I call unto him."

You can always be sure of this,...The Lord will answer when I call him.

(Psalm 4:3 KJV)

"My voice shalt thou hear in the morning, O LORD; in the morning will I direct my prayer unto thee, and will look up."

Each morning I bring my requests to you and wait expectantly.

(Psalm 5:3 KJV)

"Be still, and know that I am God: I will be exalted among the heathen, I will be exalted in the earth."

Be silent, and know that I am God…

Being quiet helps us hear God's voice.

(Psalm 46:10 KJV)

"And after the earthquake a fire; but the LORD was not in the fire: and after the fire a still small voice."

God is big, so we anticipate that him would speak with the voice of thunder or lightning or tremor (earthquake) or fire. Be that as it may, God often expresses his ground-breaking love in gentle whispers. Tune in for God's whispers as well as his shouts.

(I Kings 19:12 KJV)

PROMISE FROM GOD

"Turn you at my reproof: behold, I will pour out my spirit unto you, I will make known my words unto you."

Come here and listen to me! I'll pour out the spirit of wisdom upon you and make you wise.

(Proverbs 1:2 KJV 3)

LONELINESS

188. I'm lonely. What can I do?

"Yea, thou I walk through the valley of the shadow of death, I will fear no evil: for thou art with me; thy rod and thy staff they comfort me."

(Psalm 23:4 KJV)

"For the mountains shall depart, and the hills be removed; but my kindness shall not depart from thee, neither shall the covenant of my peace be removed, saith the LORD that hath mercy on thee."

Perceive that you are not unlovable or insufficient in light of the fact that you are lonely.

You have value because God made you, loves you, and promises never to leave you.

(Isaiah 54:10 KJV)

"And they met Moses and Aaron, who stood in the way, as they came forth from Pharaoh:"

'And they said unto them, The LORD look upon you, and judge; because ye have made our savour to be abhorred in the eyes of Pharaoh, and in the eyes of his servants, to put a sword in their hand to slay us."

"And Moses returned unto the LORD, and said, Lord, wherefore hast thou so evil entreated this people? Why is it that thou hast sent me?

"For since I came to Pharaoh to speak in thy name, he hath done evil to this people; neither hast thou delivered thy people at all."

Do not to abandon God when you are lonely. This will make you feel frustrated about yourself, become discouraged, and fall prey to temptation.

(Exodus 5:20-23 KJV)

"Now when John had heard in the prison the works of Christ, he sent two of his disciples,"

"And said unto him, Art thou he that should come, or do we look for another?"

(Matthew 11:2, 3 KJV)

"Wherefore let them that suffer according to the will of God commit the keeping of their souls to him in well doing, as unto a faithful Creator."

Sometimes we feel alone in our representing Christ. We can breathe easy in light of realizing that there are other people who are equally committed and that God rewards our bold and faithful commitment.

(I Peter 4:19 KJV)

"So we, being many, are one body in Christ, and every one members one of another."

Put yourself in traffic. Get involved in a local church.

(Romans 12:5 KJV)

"Fear thou not; for I am with thee: be not dismayed; for I am thy God: I will strengthen thee; yea, I will help thee; yea, I will uphold thee with the right hand of my righteousness."

God will uphold us with his righteous, victorious hand.

(Isaiah 41:10 KJV)

"LET not your heart be troubled: ye believe in God, believe also in me."

Don't be troubled. You trust God, now trust in me.

(John 14:1 KJV)

189. Has everyone deserted me?

"And Moses spake before the LORD, saying, Behold, the children of Israel have not hearkened unto me; how then shall Pharaoh hear me, who am of uncircumcised lips?

But LORD! Moses objected. My own people won't listen to me anymore...

(Exodus 6:12 KJV)

"When my father and my mother forsake me, then the LORD will take me up."

Even though my father or mother abandon me, the LORD will hold me close.

(Psalm 27:10 KJV)

"A man that hath friends must shew himself friendly; and there is a friend that sticketh closer than a brother."

There are many "friends" who destroy each other, but a real and true friend sticks closer than a brother."

(Proverbs 18:24 KJV)

"Be strong and of a good courage, fear not, nor be afraid of them: for the LORD thy God, he it is that doth go with thee; he will not fail thee; nor forsake thee."

God will never fail not forsake you!

(Deuteronomy 31:6 KJV)

"The eternal God is thy refuge, and underneath are the everlasting arms: and he shall trust out the enemy from before thee; and shall say, Destroy them."

God is your refuge, and his everlasting arms are under you. He thrusts out the enemy before you...

(Deuteronomy 33:27 KJV)

"He healeth the broken in heart, and bindeth up their wounds."

(Psalm 147:3 KJV)

190. How can I help those who are lonely?

"I have no greater joy than to hear that my children walk in truth.'

"Beloved, thou doest faithfully whatsoever thou doest to the brethren, and to strangers;"

"Which have borne witness of thy charity before the church: whom if thou bring forward on their journey after a godly sort, thou shalt do well:"

"Because that for his name's sake they went forth, taking nothing of the Gentiles."

"We therefore ought to receive such, that we might be fellowhelpers to the truth."

You are doing a good work for God when you take care of the traveling teachers who are passing through...

(III John 1:5-8 KJV)

"Pure religion and undefiled before God and the Father is this, To visit the fatherless and widows in their affliction, and to keep himself unspotted from the world."

We must care for orphans and widows in their troubles.

(James 1:27 KJV)

PROMISE FROM GOD

"Let your conversation be without covetousness; and be content with such things as ye have: for he hath said, I WILL NEVER LEAVE THEE, NOR FORSAKE THEE."=

(Hebrews 13:5 KJV)

LOSS

191. How do I deal with loss in my life?

"Now Jesus was not yet come into the town, but was in that place where Martha met him."

"The Jews then which were with her in the house, and comforted her, when they saw Mary, that she rose up hastily and went out, followed her, saying, She goeth unto the grave to weep there."

"Then when Mary was come where Jesus was, and saw him, she fell down at his feet, saying unto him, Lord, if thou hadst been here, my brother had not died."

"When Jesus therefore saw her weeping, and the Jews also weeping which came with her, he groaned in the spirit, and was troubled,"

"And said, Where have ye laid him? They said unto him, Lord, come and see."

"Jesus wept."

"Then said the Jews, Behold how he loved him!"

Don't deny your loss. Great distress is the consequence of great love. The tears of Jesus at Lazarus' passing everlastingly validate our tears of grief.

(John 11:30-36 KJV)

"AND Joseph fell upon his father's face, and wept upon him, and kissed him."

"And Joseph commanded his servants the physicians to embalm his father: and the physicians embalmed Israel."

"And forty days were fulfilled for him; for so are fulfilled the days of those which are embalmed: and the Egyptians mourned for him threescore and ten days."

"And when the days of his mourning were past, Joseph spake unto the house of Pharaoh, saying, If now I have found grace in your eyes, speak, I pray you, in the ears of Pharaoh, saying,"

"My father made me swear, saying, Lo, I die: in my grave which I have digged for me in the land of

Ca'-naan, there shalt thou bury me. Now therefore let me go up, I pray thee, and bury my father, and I will come again."

"And Pharaoh said, Go up, and bury thy father, according as he made thee swear."

"And Joseph went up to bury his father; and with him went up all the servants of Pharaoh, the elders of his house, and all the elders of the land of Egypt,"

"And all the house of Joseph, and his brethren, and his father's house: only their little ones, and their flocks and their herds, they left in the land of Go'-shen."

"And there went up with him both chariots and horsemen: and it was a very great company."

"And they came to the threshingfloor of A'-tad, which is beyond Jordan, and there they mourned with a great and very sore lamentation: and he made a mourning for his father seven days."

"And when the inhabitants of the land, the Ca'-nann-ites, saw the mourning in the floor of A'-tad, they said, This is a grievous mourning to the Egyptians: wherefore the name of it was called A'-bel-miz'-ra-im, which is beyond Jordan."

"And his sons did unto him according as he commanded them:"

"For his sons carried him into the land of Canaan, and buried him in the cave of the field of Mach-pe'-lah, which Abraham bought with the field for a possession of a buryingplace of E'-phron the Hit'-tite, before Mam'-re."

There was a time of national grieving for seventy days...

Grief is a procedure that must not be denied or rushed. The ceremonies of wakes, visitations, funeral services, and remembrance benefits all assist us with traveling through the phases of grief (loss).

(Genesis 50:1-13 KJV)

"AND it came to pass, after the year was expired, at the time when kings go forth to battle, that David sent Jo'-ab, and his servants with him, and all Israel; and they destroyed the children of Ammon, and besieged Rab'-bah. But David tarried still at Jerusalem."

"And it came to pass in an eveningtide, that David arose from off his bed, and walked upon the roof of the king's house: and from the roof he saw a woman washing herself; and the woman was very beautiful to look upon."

"And David sent and enquired after the woman. And one said, Is not this Bath-she'-ba, the daughter of E'li'-am, the wife of U-ri'-ah the Hit'-tite?"

"And David sent messengers, and took her; and she came in unto him, and he lay with her; for she was purified from her uncleanness: and she returned unto her house."

"And the woman conceived, and sent and told David, and said, I am with child."

For reasons not so much known, king David surrendered the dynamic authority (leadership) of his soldiers. The misfortune may have made a vacuum in his life that he was looking to load up with a shameless relationship with Bathsheba. As we lament our misfortunes we should be mindful so as not to "medicate" our pain with that which will just make more pain.

(II Samuel 11:1-5 KJV)

"And there came a messenger unto Job, and said, The oxen were plowing, and the asses feeding beside them:"

"And the Sa-be'-ans fell upon them, and took them away; yea, they have slain the servants with the edge of the sword; and I only am escaped alone to tell thee."

"While he was yet speaking, there came also another, and said, the fire of God is fallen from heaven, and hath burned up the sheep, and the servants, and consumed them; and I only am escaped alone to tell thee."

"While he was yet speaking, there came also another, and said, The Chal-de'-ans made out three bands, and fell upon the camels, and have carried them away, yea, and slain the servants with the edge of the sword; and I only am escaped alone to tell thee."

"While he was yet speaking, there came also another, and said, Thy sons and thy daughters were eating and drinking wine in their eldest brother's house:"

"And behold, there came a great wind from the wilderness, and smote the four corners of the house and it fell upon the young men, and they are dead; and I only am escaped alone to tell thee."

"Then Job arose, and rent his mantle, and shaved his head, and fell down upon the ground, and worshipped,"

"And said, Naked came I out of my mother's womb, and naked shall I return thither: the LORD gave, and the LORD hath taken away; blessed be the name of the LORD."

"In all this Job sinned not, nor charged God foolishly."

Misfortunes (losses) continually bring pain. perceiving and communicating that pain is neither wrong nor sinful, but instead a sound articulation of how God created us.

(Job 1:14-2 KJV 2)

192. I feel like I've lost everything. Where can I turn?

"Yea, though I walk through the valley of the shadow of death, I will fear no evil: for thou art with me; thy rod and thy staff they comfort me."

In the darkness of grief we can turn to the Lord, who promises his comfort and strength.

(Psalm 23:4 KJV)

"He is despised and rejected of men; a man of sorrows, and acquainted with grief; and we hid as it were our faces from him; he was despised, and we esteemed him not."

"Surely he hath borne our grief, and carried our sorrows: yet we did esteem him stricken, smitten of God and afflicted."

"But he was wounded for our transgressions, he was bruised for our iniquities: the chastisement of our peace was upon him; and with his stripes we are healed."

"All we like sheep have gone astray; we have turned every one to his own way; and the LORD hath laid on him the iniquity of us all."

"He was oppressed, and he was afflicted, yet he brought as a lamb to the slaughter, and as sheep before her shearers is dumb, so he openeth not his mouth."

Yet it was our weakness he carried; it was our sorrows that weighed him down.

God demonstrates his love for us by being willing to experience all our griefs and sorrows.

(Isaiah 53:3-7 KJV)

"Blessed be God, even the Father of our Lord Jesus Christ, the Father of mercies, and the God of all comfort;"

"Who comforteth us in all our tribulation, that we may be able to comfort them which are in any trouble, by the comfort wherewith we ourselves are comforted of God."

"For as the sufferings of Christ abound in us, so our consolation also aboundeth by Christ."

"And whether we be afflicted, it is for your consolation and salvation, which is effectual in the enduring of the same sufferings which we also suffer: or whether we be comforted, it is for your consolation and salvation."

"And our hope of you is stedfast, knowing, that as ye are partakers of the sufferings, so shall ye be also of the consolation."

(II Corinthians 1:3-7 KJV)

193. Are there any losses that are for our good?

"Though I might also have confidence in the flesh. If any other man thinketh that he hath whereof he might trust in the flesh, I more."

"Circumcised the eighth day, of the stock of Israel, of the tribe of Benjamin, an Hebrew of the Hebrews; as touching the law, a Pharisee;"

"Concerning zeal, persecuting the church; touching the righteousness which is in the law, blameless."

"But what things were gain to me, those I counted loss for Christ."

"Yea, doubtless, and I count all things but loss for the excellency of the knowledge of Christ Jesus my Lord: for whom I have suffered the loss of all things, and do count them but dung, that I may win Christ."

"And be found in him, not having mine own righteousness, which is of the law, but that which is through the faith of Christ, the righteousness which is of God by faith:"

"That I may know him, and the power of his resurrection, and the fellowship of his sufferings, being made comformable unto his death;"

To know the power of Christ in our lives we should be happy to relinquish all our self-importance and pride.

(Philippians 3:4-11 KJV)

"Mortify therefore your members which are upon the earth; fornication, uncleanness, inordinate affection, evil concupiscence, and covetousness, which is idolatry:"

"For which things' sake the wrath of God cometh on the children of disobedience:"

"In the which ye also walked some time, when ye lived in them."

"But now ye also put off all these; anger, wrath, malice, blasphemy, filthy communication out of your mouth."

"Lie not one to another, seeing that ye have put off the old man with his deeds;"

When we give our hearts and lives to Jesus Christ, we should regard (treat) our previous lifestyles (the old man) as though they were dead and gone!

(Colossians 3:5-9 KJV)

PROMISE FROM GOD

"The LORD is nigh unto them that are of a broken heart; and saveth such as be of a contrite spirit."

The Lord is close to the brokenhearted; he rescues those who are crushed in spirit.

(Proverbs 1:2 KJV 3)

LOVE

194. Must I love other people? What if I don't want to?

"A new commandment I give unto you, That ye love one another; as I have loved you, that ye also love one another."

(John 13:34 KJV)

"He that saith he is in the light, and hateth his brother, is in darkness even until now."

Anyone who says, "I am in the light" but rejects another Christian is still in darkness.

(I John 2:9 KJV)

""By this shall all men know that ye are my disciples, if ye have love one to another."

(John 13:35 KJV)

"And above all things have fervent charity among yourselves; for CHARITY SHALL COVER THE MULTITUDE OF SINS."

(I Peter 4:8 KJV)

"No man hath seen God at any time. If we love one another, God dwelleth in us, and his love is perfected in us."

Being a Christian comes with certain expectations, and one of them is that we will love others. Our Christian conduct is verification concerning whether we love one another, and loving each other is evidence (proof) that we belong to Christ.

(I John 4:12 KJV)

195. What are some special things that come from a loving relationship?

"Hatred stirreth up strifes: but love coverth all sins."

Hatred stirs up fighting, but love covers all offenses.

(Proverbs 10:12 KJV)

"Charity suffereth long, and is kind; charity envieth not; charity vaunteth not itself, is not puffed up,"

"Doth not behave itself unseemly, seeketh not her own, is not easily provoked, thinketh no evil;"

"Rejoiceth not in iniquity, but rejoiceth in the truth;"

"Beareth all things, believeth all things, hopeth all things, endureth all things."

(I Corinthians 13:4-7 KJV)

The gifts that come from love are many. Here are a few as follows:

(1) Forgiveness
(2) Patience
(3) Kindness
(4) Love For Truth
(5) Love For Justice
(6) Love For The Best In A Person
(7) Loyalty At Any Cost
(8) Belief In A Person No Matter What.

Love Does Not Allow For:

(1) Jealousy
(2) Envy
(3) Pride
(4) A Haughty Spirit
(5) Selfishness

(6) Rudeness
(7) A Demand For One's Own Way
(8) Irritability
(9) Grudges

196. Does God really love me? How can I know?

"And I will betroth thee unto me for ever; yea, I will betroth thee unto me in righterousness, and in judgment, and in lovingkindness, and in mercies."

"I will make you my wife forever, showing you righteousness and justice, unfailing love and compassion."

(Hosea 2:19 KJV)

"For God so loved the world, that he gave his only begotten Son, that whosoever believeth in him should not perish, but have everlasting life."

(John 3:16 KJV)

"Beloved, let us love one another: for love is of God; and every one that loveth is born of God, and knoweth God."

"He that loveth not knoweth not God; for God is love."

"In this way manifested the love of God toward us, because that God sent his only begotten Son into the world, that we might live through him."

"Herein is love, not that we loved God, but that he loved us, and sent his Son to be the propitiation for our sins."

"Beloved, if God so loved us, we ought also to love one another."

"No man hath seen God at any time. If we love one another, God dwelleth in us, and his love is perfected in us."

(I John 4:7-12 KJV)

"And hope maketh not ashamed; because the love of God is shed abroad in our hearts by the Holy Ghost which is given unto us."

(Romans 5:5 KJV)

"Who shall separate us from the love of Christ? Shall tribulation, or distress, or persecution, or famine, or nakedness, or peril, or sword?"

"As it is written, FOR THY SAKE WE ARE KILLED ALL THE DAY LONG; WE ARE ACCOUNTED AS SHEEP FOR THE SLAUGHTER."

"Nay, in all these things we are more than conquerors through him that loved us."

For I am persuaded, that neither death, nor life, nor angels, nor principalities, nor powers, nor things present, nor things to come,"

"Nor height, nor depth, nor any other creature, shall be able to separate us from the love

of God, which is in Christ Jesus our Lord."

(Romans 8:35-39 KJV)

197. How should we show our love to God?

"And whosoever shall give to drink unto one of these little ones a cup of cold water only in the name of a disciple, verily I say unto you, he shall in no wise lose his reward."

By showing our love to needy people whom God loves.

(Matthew 10:4 KJV 2)

"He that hath my commandments, and keepeth them, he it is that loveth me: and he that loveth me shall be loved of my Father, and I will love him, and will manifest myself to him."

By obeying Him.

(John 14:21 KJV)

"So when they had dined, Jesus saith to Simon Peter, Simon, son of Jo'-nas, lovest thou me more than these? He saith unto him, Yea, Lord; thou knowest that I love thee. He saith unto him, Feed my lambs.'

"He saith to him again the second time, Simon, son of Jo'-nas, lovest thou me? He saith unto him, Yea, Lord; thou knowest that I love thee. He saith unto him, Feed my sheep."

"He saith unto him the third time, Simon, son of Jo'-nas, lovest thou me? Peter was grieved because he said unto him the third time, Lovest thou me? And he said unto him, Lord, thou knowest all things; thou knowest that I love thee. Jesus saith unto him, Feed my sheep."

Do you love me?...feed my lambs...take care of my sheep...feed my sheep.

(John 21:15-17 KJV)

"For God is not unrighteous to forget your work and labour of love, which ye have shewed toward his name, in that ye have ministered to the saints, and do minister."

He will not forget...how you have shown your love to him by caring for other Christians.

By guiding and helping Jesus' followers.

(Hebrews 6:10 KJV)

"I WAS glad when they said unto me, Let us go into the house of the LORD."

By worshiping him and praising him for his love to us.

(Psalm 122:1 KJV)

PROMISE FROM GOD

"Nor height, nor depth, nor any other creature, shall be able to separate us from the love of God, which is in Christ Jesus our Lord."

Regardless of whether we are high over the sky or in the most profound (deepest part of the sea) sea, nothing in all creation will ever have the option to separate us from the love of God that is revealed in Christ Jesus our Lord.

(Romans 8:39 KJV)

LOYALTY

198. Why is loyalty important?

"All the paths of the LORD are mercy and truth unto such as keep his covenant and his testimonies."

Loyal obedience to God brings a sweet scent (fragrance) into our lives because we are full of love and truth.

(Psalm 25:10 KJV)

"And they lifted up their voice, and wept again: and Or'-pah kissed her mother in law; but Ruth clave unto her."

'And she said, Behold, they sister in law is gone back unto her people, and unto her gods: return thou after thy sister in law."

"And Ruth said, Intreat me not to leave thee, or to return from following after thee: for whither thou goest, I will go; and where thou lodgest, I will lodge: thy people shall be my people, and thy God my God:"

Loyalty is the mark of true friendship.

(Ruth 1:14-16 KJV)

"Beareth all things, believeth all things, hopeth all things, endureth all things."

Love never gives up, never loses faith, is always hopeful, and endures through every circumstance.

(I Corinthians 13:7 KJV)

199. What kind of people are loyal people?

"The integrity of the upright shall guide them: but the perverseness of transgressors shall destroy them."

Good people are guided by their honesty.

A loyal person is trustworthy, and therefore honest.

(Proverbs 11:3 KJV)

"A friend loveth at all times, and a brother is born for adversity."

A friend is always loyal, honest, and a brother is born to help in time of need.

True friends are loyal.

(Proverbs 17:17 KJV)

200. Can you have divided loyalty?

"No servant can serve two masters: for either he will hate the one, and love the other; or else he will hold to the one, and despise the other. Ye cannot serve God and mammon."

Loyalty, by definition, is undeviating commitment. If you claim loyalty to God, you cannot also claim loyalty to anything that takes priority over God.

(Luke 16:13 KJV)

PROMISE FROM GOD

"O love the LORD, all ye his saints: for the LORD preseerveth the faithful, and plentifully rewardeth the proud doer.

Those who are loyal to the LORD he protects.

(Psalm 31:23 KJV)

Bibliography

The Holy Bible (1964) Authorized King James Version. Chicago, Ill.: J. G. Ferguson

The Holy Bible (1982) New International Version. Grand Rapids, MI.: Thomas Nelson (Used By Permission)

The Holy Bible (1978) New York, NY.: New York International Bible Society (Used By Permission)

The Holy Bible (1953) The Revised Standard Version. Nashville, TN.: Thomas Nelson & Sons (Used By Permission)

The Holy Bible (1901) The American Standard Version. Nashville, TN.: Thomas Nelson (Used By Permission)

The Holy Bible (1959) The Berkeley Version. Grand Rapids, MI.: Zondervan (Used By Permission)

The Holy Bible (1977) The New American Standard Bible. USA.: The Lockman Foundation (Used By Permission)

The Holy Bible (1996) The New Living Translation. Wheaton, Ill.: Tyndale House Publishers (Used By Permission)

The New Testament In The Language Of The People (1937, 1949) Chicago, Ill.: Charles B. Williams, Bruce Humphries, Inc, The Moody Bible Institute (Used By Permission)

The New Testament In Modern English (1958) New York, NY.: J. B. Phillips, Macmillan (Used By Permission)
The Wycliff Bible Commentary (1962, 1968) Nashville, TN.: Chicago, Ill.: The Southwestern Company, The Moody Bible Institute Of Chicago

About The Author

The Reverend Dr. John Thomas Wylie is one who has dedicated his life to the work of God's Service, the service of others; and being a powerful witness for the Gospel of Our Lord and Savior Jesus Christ. Dr. Wylie was called into the Gospel Ministry June 1979, whereby in that same year he entered The American Baptist College of the American Baptist Theological Seminary, Nashville, Tennessee.

As a young Seminarian, he read every book available to him that would help him better his understanding of God as well as God's plan of Salvation and the Christian Faith. He made a commitment as a promising student that he would inspire others as God inspires him. He understood early in his ministry that we live in times where people question not only who God is; but whether miracles are real, whether or not man can make a change, and who the enemy is or if the enemy truly exists.

Dr. Wylie carried out his commitment to God, which has been one of excellence which led to his earning his Bachelors of Arts in Bible/Theology/Pastoral

Studies. Faithful and obedient to the call of God, he continued to matriculate in his studies earning his Masters of Ministry from Emmanuel Bible College, Nashville, Tennessee & Emmanuel Bible College, Rossville, Georgia. Still, inspired to please the Lord and do that which is well – pleasing in the Lord's sight, Dr. Wylie recently on March 2006, completed his Masters of Education degree with a concentration in Instructional Technology earned at The American Intercontinental University, Holloman Estates, Illinois. Dr. Wylie also previous to this, earned his Education Specialist Degree from Jones International University, Centennial, Colorado and his Doctorate of Theology from The Holy Trinity College and Seminary, St. Petersburg, Florida.

Dr. Wylie has served in the capacity of pastor at two congregations in Middle Tennessee and Southern Tennessee, as well as served as an Evangelistic Preacher, Teacher, Chaplain, Christian Educator, and finally a published author, writer of many great inspirational Christian Publications such as his first publication:

"Only One God: Who Is He?" – published August 2002 via formally 1st books library (which is now AuthorHouse Book Publishers located in Bloomington, Indiana & Milton Keynes, United Kingdom) which caught

the attention of The Atlanta Journal Constitution Newspaper.

Dr. Wylie is happily married to Angel G. Wylie, a retired Dekalb Elementary School teacher who loves to work with the very young children and who always encourages her husband to move forward in the Name of Jesus Christ. They have Four children, 11 grand-children and one great-grandson all of whom they are very proud. Both Dr. Wylie and Angela Wylie serve as members of the Salem Baptist Church, located in Lilburn, Georgia, where the Reverend Dr. Richard B. Haynes is Senior pastor.

Dr. Wylie has stated of his wife: "she knows the charm and beauty of sincerity, goodness, and purity through Jesus Christ. Yes, she is a Christian and realizes the true meaning of loveliness as the reflection as her life of holy living gives new meaning, hope, and purpose to that of her husband, her children, others may say of her, "Behold the handmaiden of the Lord." A Servant of Jesus Christ!

Printed in the United States
By Bookmasters